SPA STYLE

ARABIA

THERAPIES • CUISINES • SPAS

SPA STYLE
ARABIA

DAVID VAN DER MEULEN

KATE O'BRIEN

Thames & Hudson

First published in the United Kingdom in 2006 by
Thames & Hudson Ltd, 181A High Holborn,
London WC1V 7QX

www.thamesandhudson.com

© 2006 Bolding Books
Design and Layout © 2006 Editions Didier Millet

British Library Cataloguing-in-Publication Data
A catalogue record for this book is available from the British
Library

ISBN-13: 978-0-500-28621-0

ISBN-10: 0-500-28621-3

Printed and bound in Singapore

Before following any advice or practice contained in this book,
it is recommended that you consult your doctor. The publisher
cannot accept responsibility for any injuries or damage incurred
as a result of following any of the suggestions, preparations
or procedures described in this book, or by using any of the
therapeutic methods that are mentioned.

Every effort has been made to ensure the accuracy of the
information in this book at the time of going to press. Some
details are liable to change and the publisher recommends
calling ahead to verify information with the respective
properties.

The authors would like to thank the following for their help and
contribution: Jean Paul Naquin, Christian Gradnitzer,
Dr Lamees Hamdan, Nadine Skaff, Trevor Studd and Anni Hood.

Contents

Introduction

Spa Style Arabia is the essential and authoritative guide to Arabian spa culture delving into the myriad of richly diverse cultures from Ancient Egypt (the land of the pharaohs) to Turkey, Persia (Iran), the Levant region (Jordan and Lebanon) and Morocco in Northern Africa. More than a destination, the Middle East is a cradle of some of the world's oldest and most mysterious civilizations and a compilation of customs that are so vivid, deep and varied. Teeming with life, Arabia is incessantly vibrant with a common denominator of luxury and opulence that blankets today's resorts, hotels and day spas. From the mighty monuments of Cairo, to a languid cruise along the River Nile, from Dubai's ostentatious hotels to the stark, unchanging calm of the vast open desert, Arabia is indeed a land of astoundingly absurd contrasts.

Until relatively recently, traditional medicine was the only type of medicine available to a large section of people of the Arabian region. There were only a few schools of formal training and—like many other countries in the East—skills and recipes were simply handed down from one generation to the next. The following pages offer an insight into these time-honoured practises. Many of these traditions are derived from the Arabian 'Prince of Physicians', Abu Ali ibn Sina, who to this day is rated as one of the most highly gifted scholars in the history of medicine. Today,

with social cultures constantly evolving and changing and the introduction of Western-style therapies, there is even more of a need to preserve these ancient healing therapies that served the region for centuries.

The following pages will take you on a spa journey enabling you to relive the legend of Cleopatra as ancient milk bath rituals, and the hammam and rasul experiences are explained. These ancient therapies are today combined with more decadent precious stone and crushed gem therapies, as well as the modern practises of aromatherapy and first-class facial treatments. Also, growing in popularity is to tap into the body's innate healing with massages using coloured gem stones such as rose quartz, emerald and diamond. From therapies, the cuisine chapter provides recipes for culinary delights from some of the world's most luxurious and lavish resorts. Each offers a sumptuous choice of exotic ingredients and healthy and fresh meals, covering opulent, fusion, modern Arabian and pan-Arabian cuisines. Spa Digest provides essential information on the region's best spas.

Spa Style Arabia unravels the mystery, allowing you to discover not only the roots of today's most popular therapies and where to experience them, but also how to enjoy an authentic Arabian spa treatment in the privacy of your own home.

Spa Therapies

Built in grandeur, many of Arabia's spas offer the opulence of ancient Arabia with up-to-the-minute therapies enabling the client to taste, touch and feel the difference. From classic cures with indigenous ingredients such as henna, honey, dates and the eternally enduring rose, to more sophisticated rituals based on precious stones and crystals, the Spa Therapies chapter demystifies the legends and demonstrates how these ancient rituals have become intricately linked with the modern spa experience. With so many Arabian-inspired therapies springing up in spa menus worldwide today it's easy to forget that in the beginning, scented products were reserved exclusively for religious rituals.

Deepen your appreciation of the Arabian spa, learn how the traditional healing systems of the Hakims are still well and truly alive in the modern Arabian spa and endeavour to experience, in Arabia, or in the home, the exotic blend of time-honoured and truly unmatched natural therapies to soothe and enrich body, mind and spirit.

The Origins of Arabian Medicine

ANCIENT INNOVATIONS

During the Dark Ages, when science was close to Barbarism in the West, it has been said that the Hakims (doctors or 'wise men') of the Muslim world made discoveries that changed medicine forever—from the introduction of caesarean sections and the induction of anaesthesia by inhalation, to the first complicated eye surgery, operating on head fractures and performing dental surgery (such as the insertion of false teeth made from the bones of animals). They gave vivid clinical descriptions of several diseases allowing for the diagnosis of a number of illnesses such as measles, smallpox, meningitis and hay fever.

Much of the success of Arabian medicine is attributed to their endorsement of Greek and Roman medicine. Most notably, the works of Hippocrates (460-360 BC), often referred to as the father of medicine, and Claudius Galen (131-210 AD) have been credited as forming the backbone of Arabian medicine during the Middles Ages.

Hippocrates constructed a theoretical foundation for medicine that survived until the 16th century. Fundamental to this was the idea that health and illness are the results of harmony—or disharmony—of the four humours (yellow bile, black bile, phlegm and blood), their respective qualities (choleric, melancholic, phlegmatic and sanguineous), their natures (hot, dry, humid and cold) and the seasons. To this day diagnosis of a disease or condition Arabian-style rests on the evaluation of these parameters among others. Much like in traditional Chinese medicine (TCM), ayurveda and other Eastern philosophies, when these forces are in balance, there is health and harmony. However, this dynamic equilibrium is easily disrupted by forces from within, such as emotional upset, and external environmental factors, that leave the body more susceptible to illness and disease.

THIS PAGE: Fresh fruit is in abundance in the spas across Arabia.
LEFT: The Arabian desert inspires calm with its vibrant colours and intense silence.
PAGE 10: Hot stone therapy is offered in many spas in the region.

The human body contains blood, phlegm, yellow bile and black bile. These are the things that make up its constitution and cause its pain and health. Health is primarily that state in which these constituent substances are in correct proportion to each other both in strength and quality and are mixed well. Pain occurs when one of the substances presents either in deficiency or an excess or is separated in the body and not mixed with the others.

Hippocrates

With the collapse of the Roman Empire around 475 AD and the repeated sacking of the great library in Alexandria (where key medical texts were archived) the works of these great scholars, Hippocrates and Galen, were lost to the West. However, the knowledge lived on in Arabic translations in the East, at the same time the early foundations of Arabian folk medicine had already adopted the concept that "for every malady Allah has appointed an appropriate remedy".

The combination of the traditional and modern medical approaches, and the growing astrological influence flooding in from India and the Far East, formed the blueprint for Arabian medicine as it became better known from that time onwards. Indeed, the influence of food, the humours and the elements remained paramount predictors of health and the potential basis of cures.

Independent Arabic medical literature started to appear in the 9th century, reaching its prime in the 11th century with many physicians possessing remarkable powers of medical diagnosis through external signs and symptoms.

The field of ophthalmology received special attention in Egypt in particular, due to its prevalence of eye diseases, and Arabian physicians described in detail the anatomy and physiology of the eye and the causes of many eye diseases. Consequently many of the Latin terms used in ophthalmology are of Arabic origin.

As with other Eastern philosophies, Arabic medicine was more concerned with prevention rather than cure. Diet and bathing were considered the most important tools in the prevention of disease among the Hakims. They also mastered a range of drugs both naturally occurring and chemically

THIS PAGE: The influence of food has been recognized from the beginning of Arabian medicine. This ancient wall painting shows men picking dates, a well-loved fruit that is cherished for its healing properties.
OPPOSITE: Cleanliness, along with a healthy diet, was an imperative part of the prevention of illness. Bathhouses were a common sight in ancient Arabia.

formed. They included ambergris, cassia, clovers, mercury, myrrh, nutmeg, sienna and sandalwood, which, along with analgesics such as opium, poppy, cannabis and camphor, were prescribed to re-balance both body and mind.

Respected by medical scholars to this day is Abu Ali ibn Sina (circa 937–1037), known as the 'Prince of Physicians' or Avicenna in the West. Writing over 100 books in his lifetime, this gifted scholar's most famous work, *The Canon of Medicine* (*al-Qanun fi'l-Tibb*) has been credited as the single most influential work in the history of medicine.

The *Canon of Medicine* was the definitive codification of all Greco-Arabic (or Unani-Tibb) medicine and became half of the medical curriculum for the European universities in the latter part of the 15th century. As well as organizing existing medical knowledge, ibn Sina made new observations of his own including the discovery of meningitis, the manner of the spread of epidemics and the contagious properties of tuberculosis. He also wrote a book dedicated entirely to the rose, the flower most cherished by Islam (see page 16).

However, it was not until the 12th century that Latin translations of major Arabic works started to appear in Europe, with Arabian medicine achieving an almost mythical status among European physicians. Abu Ali ibn Sina and the works of Al Razi Rhazes (circa 950 AD) soon became the authoritative texts on the teachings of medicine in Europe. Even today, the image of the Hakim, with his gold and silver brocaded turban and halo of intellect curiously appears in medical textbooks—testament to the unqualified respect that has been bestowed on these physician-philosophers throughout the centuries.

THIS PAGE (FROM TOP): Stylish detail in an Arabian spa; rosebuds are a luxurious addition to a milk bath, the rosewater will soften the skin.
OPPOSITE: As well as adding rose petals, add a few drops of essential oil of rose, or attar of rose; the heat will help the skin absorb the oils.

The Rose

The great physician Avicenna (Abu Ali ibn Sina) is credited with having distilled the first rose oil, the first flower ever distilled, around the 10ᵗʰ century in Persia. Traditionally associated with Venus the Goddess of Love and Beauty, it is no surprise that the rose holds the richest and most complex symbolism associated with any plant in the scholars alchemy. It was an essential part of materia medica in the Middle Ages and endured for centuries, being used for a range of problems from digestive and menstrual headaches to nervous tension, eye infections and skin complaints.

Before distillation or extraction, rose petals were put in water to make rosewater and in oil to make rose oil. In ancient Persia, rosewater was used to purify the mosque. It was also used to scent gloves, flavour sweet delicacies and was sprinkled on guests from a glass flask called a 'gulabdan'. Rose petals, saffron, and mahlab (a yellow seed similar to sesame) were ground into a powder and used to make a fragrant body powder while prayer beads were made from Arabic gum and rose petals which released their scent when held. It has been said that often such a large quantity of rosewater was produced that canals were filled with it and on hot sunny days an oily scum would rise to the surface and

be captured in small vials and became the original attar of rose (rose oil). In the early 1600s the Turks introduced the Rose industry to Bulgaria where, to this day, the town of Kazanlik remains home to the best rose plantations and a superior quality attar of rose.

Two varieties of rose are now used commercially for the production of attar of rose: rosa centifolia and rosa damascena, with slight variations in colour and aroma (from a greenish-orange to a deep browny-red). The rose, the queen of flowers, has an extraordinarily complex oil, with over 300 known constituents and is often considered the queen among essential oils. Most essential oils have a therapeutic affinity with a particular organ in the body and the rose, with its feminine qualities, is believed to have a powerful effect on the uterus. As a cleansing, purifying and adaptable oil, it helps regulate the menstrual cycle, reduce excessive menstrual loss and promote conception. On an emotional level, rose oil acts as a gentle but potent antidepressant and is especially helpful where an emotional disturbance is linked to female sexuality or the reproductive cycle. Also considered an aphrodisiac, the rose has widely been used in wedding ceremonies. The ancient Romans scattered rose petals on the bridal bed—a wedding tradition that is still in existence.

Rosewater and oil are widely used in skincare especially for dry, sensitive or ageing skin. It helps diminish enlarged capillaries or thread veins on the face while also acting as an effective antiseptic for eye infections. To this day, in spas across Arabia and increasingly in other parts of the world, the rose is an essential part of the overall indulgence. For example, the exquisite Shiffa Rose Heaven Experience at the Six Senses Spa at Madinat Jumeirah in Dubai lavishly utilizes the many facets of the flower—using a rose steam, rosewater and incense, Rose of Damascus Luxury Body Polish, 1001 Roses Luxury Milk Bath—in a full body massage and bathing experience.

Well-Being Beginnings

FIRST ARABIAN THERAPIES

Arabian beauty therapies date as far back as 7000 BC when the fatty oils of olive and sesame were combined with fragrant plants to create the original Neolithic ointments. Egyptian priests were the first perfumers to develop incense, aromatic oils and scented unguents (thick, pleasant-smelling oily substances for the skin) for use in the temples. The Hebrews also burned incense with their sacrifices, using anointing oils as part of their rituals and myrrh for purification ceremonies.

Although priests of all religions endeavoured to restrict the use of perfumes to the exclusive worship of the deities, warning against the vanity of self-adornment, opportunistic merchants were willing to sell to anyone who could afford the high prices and it was not long before royalty and nobility (and anyone else who could afford it) were indulging in fragrance. As the use of these unusually high-priced items was restricted to the exceptionally wealthy, Roman emperors became notorious for their extravagance and lavishness.

THIS PAGE: Classic wrought-iron details decorate Arabian spas and houses alike.
OPPOSITE: Opulence and luxury are prominent at the Givenchy Spa in Dubai.

THIS PAGE (FROM TOP): In keeping with floral traditions, refreshing and aromatic flower-filled baths and basins are a common sight in the spas; alabaster jars have been used for centuries, and are still quintessentially Arabian.
OPPOSITE (FROM TOP): Exclusive spa products that still use age-old ingredients; clean minimalist lines at the Six Senses Spa, create a calming ambience.

During the reign of the ruthless Egyptian Pharaoh, Khufu, builder of the Great Pyramid (circa 2700 BC), the use of fragrant herbs, oils and perfumes was clearly recorded on various papyrus manuscripts. They told of healing salves made of fragrant resins. Perhaps the most famous of these manuscripts is the 870-foot-long Ebers Papyrus that dates back to 1500 BC. The ancient document depicts more than 800 herbal prescriptions and remedies, including the widespread use of oil, honey and myrrh which—because of its effectiveness in preventing bacterial growth—was widely used for embalming.

Egypt's desire for producing incense and unguents such as myrrh, frankincense, cinnamon and cassia was to become legendary as was their love of pungent aromas. This became more evident with the amazing discovery made in the 20th century. After being sealed for more than 3,000 years, alabaster jars made of calcite (limestone), that were filled with spices such as frankincense preserved in fat and essential oils, gave off a faint odour when discovered in 1922 during the opening of King Tutankhamen's tomb.

It was during the Ottoman Empire (circa 1600–1923) that the most luxurious treatments were created, primarily for women. For example, body pastes and scrubs were made from myrrh, orange peel and almond, and were mixed with almond oil and lavishly applied over the body. A variant of this is included in Shiffa's Arabie Ancienne Body Polish. Furthering the Arabian tradition, it is part of the Velvet Nights royal experience at Dubai's Six Senses Spa at Madinat Jumeirah as well as at the Amara day spa at the Park Hyatt, Dubai.

Also in these early days, the Ottomans liberally infused oils such as rosemary and basil for both beautification purposes and for treating illnesses. It was mainly in the richer and larger cities where these ingredients were more plentiful, and where people had more time, that beauty traditions like these began to flourish.

Other Early Spa Traditions

An early form of beautification, saffron was powdered and mixed into a paste with water to make a blusher called 'ottoor zafran'. It was used to draw two lines, one on each cheek.

To relieve prickly heat skin conditions, a common complaint in the dry desert heat, the leaves of the yas tree were ground to a powder and applied over the affected area.

To treat a whole range of conditions from liver disorders to jaundice and open sores such as boils, a more extreme folk medicine called 'wasm' was practiced—the burning of an area of the body with a hot iron. This tradition is rarely performed now.

Fragrances for the Gods

At one time all herbs that were burnt as incense were simply referred to as frankincense. Today the word frankincense specifically refers to the gum resin drawn from the North African boswellia trees. The tree's milky sap hardens into yellow or brownish beads to make frankincense oil that has a fresh, slightly spicy, woody, and fruity aroma.

In ancient times, trading in frankincense was highly profitable with Arabia becoming the largest exporter. At the time, the trees in the southwest of the region provided the best quality frankincense resin. This particular Arabian province was also the seat of Queen Saba, who reportedly received all proceeds from this lucrative trade. So large was the trade that Arabia had a separate fleet of ships used exclusively for the transport of frankincense. Testament to the high regard in which frankincense was held was its role in Herod's burial— 5,000 slaves preceded the funeral carrying urns of burning frankincense that surrounded everything in a fragrant fog. Further, in 65 AD at the funeral of his wife Sabina Poppae, it is said that Emperor Nero burned all the frankincense produced in Arabia in one whole year. In Christian terms, the three holy kings believed that the most precious gifts to present to the Son of God in Bethlehem were gold, frankincense and myrrh.

Although little is known about the benefits of frankincense, the Catholic Church still uses it in its basic form during special ceremonies.

Enormous quantities of incense were used in the rituals of Egyptian priests. At Heliopolis, City of the Sun, incense was offered to the sun god in special ceremonies three times a day. Gums were burned at sunrise, myrrh at noon and a very costly blend of herbs and resins called kyphi (see opposite) was offered at sunset. The effect was said to be intoxicating and brought religious ecstasy.

Frankincense and other herbs burned as incense have strong disinfectant properties, so were ideal for

religious gatherings to prevent the transfer of disease while serving a dual role of cleansing the atmosphere in the church or temple after people have left their worries and negative energies behind.

Today, although frankincense has generally been substituted by more common healing herbs, it is still used as an astringent or antiseptic and to heal wounds, reduce inflammation and ease rheumatism. It can also be used to treat bronchitis or extreme coughing, colds, sinusitis and asthma. As a cosmetic oil, frankincense makes a great astringent or facial toner and helps to smooth wrinkles, scars and stretch marks. A few drops in an oil burner will help to ease stress and anxiety.

Other Incense from Arabia

Myrrh The reddish-brown gum resin drawn from the cammiphora bush. It is an astringent, stimulant, and carminative tonic. As a soothing antiseptic, it can relieve sore gums and mouth ulcers. With its anti-fungal properties, myrrh can ease athlete's foot and thrush. It can also help regulate menstrual cycles and ease menstrual pain. Myrrh oil blends well with frankincense and is used to ease anxieties and balance the emotions.

Kyphi The finest blend of incense which the ancient Egyptians offered their gods. The recipe for this incense mixture, encompasses 16 different herbs including frankincense, myrrh and sweet flag, and was written on the Egyptian papyrus of Ebers.

Kyphi was burned during the sunset hours in ancient Egyptian temples to usher in the night for the sun god, Ra. It was believed that Kyphi could remove the worries of the day, relax and calm the mind and induce sweet dreams. Because of its many luxurious ingredients, Kyphi was also applied to the skin to heal wounds. This ancient Egyptian incense was introduced to Europe where it became so famous that when the Greeks and Romans later marketed the first commercial perfume, they called it kyphi.

A Long and Beautiful History

ANCIENT EGYPTIAN PRACTICES

The first evidence of the use of cosmetics in ancient Egypt was around 1400 BC when three ladies of the court of Tuthmosis III were buried with costly royal funerary equipment which included two jars of an oil and lime cleansing cream.

As with other ancient civilizations, Egyptians worked hard to keep themselves beautiful by using a plethora of natural ingredients and secrets that had been passed down through generations, many of which remain to this day, such as the wide use of henna (see pages 58–59). They worked hard at keeping their hair healthy, shiny and strong using henna or a setting lotion mixture of beeswax and resin. To prevent hair from greying, a concoction of blood of a black ox or calf was boiled in oil and applied to the head to transfer the blackness of the animal to the grey hair, while the black horn of a gazelle was made into an unguent with oil to prevent grey hairs from appearing. Slightly less appealing was the use of putrid donkey's liver steeped in oil. A more common remedy used juniper berries kneaded into a paste and heated with plants and oil. The natural colouring of the plants rubbed off on the hair while the astringent properties of the junipers stimulated the scalp. A treatment for baldness was the placing of chopped lettuce on the bald patch which was believed to stimulate hair growth.

While body hair held erotic symbolism to many, razors were a common sight in bathing areas to remove excess body hair while creams were prepared from boiled or crushed bones of a bird, mixed and heated with fly dung, sycamore juice, gum and cucumber. The mixture was applied to the hair and pulled off when cold.

THIS PAGE: **Eyes are painted with kohl, sometimes from a very young age, and is an ongoing tradition that has survived for centuries.**
OPPOSITE: **Old passages and walkways evoke the sense of ancient times.**

THIS PAGE (FROM TOP): Perfume is so popular in the Middle East that bottles are commonly given as gifts with a handmade mixture of essential oils inside; the stunning lotus flower, a symbol of creation and rebirth.
OPPOSITE: Ornate bottles in an Arabian spa, with incense and perfumed lotions.

Eye paint served a dual purpose in ancient Egypt; as well as colouring the eyes it was used to treat or prevent eye disease. Made from equal quantities of kohl, green eye paint (which consisted of malachite, a green ore of copper), lapis lazuli, honey and ochre, it was mixed and applied as paint onto the eyelids. Black kohl (made of galena, a dark grey ore of lead) or green malachite were used to underline the dark Egyptian eyes. An overnight eye treatment of kohl and goose fat was used to revitalize tired eyes which were regularly soothed and washed with a mixture prepared from ground celery and hemp.

However, no matter what remedy was used, ancient Egyptians knew that nothing made the eyes brighter than falling in love as is evident from the words in an ancient love poem: "Like eye paint is my desire. When I see you, it makes my eyes sparkle."

Lips were painted red with gloss prepared from fat mixed with red ochre and applied with a brush or spatula. An early form of rouge, made of red ochre and fat with possibly some gull resin, is believed to have been prepared over 4,000 years ago—a more contemporary version of this is still marketed today.

Up to the first few centuries, Egypt was known as one of the most prominent developers of perfume. Although perfumes were actually created and mass-marketed elsewhere in the ancient world, it was Egypt that was most renowned and identified with a strong and successful fragrance trade. The country so identified with perfume that, during Julius Caesar's triumphs, perfume bottles were tossed to the crowd to demonstrate his mastery over Egypt.

Beautifully scented flowers were readily accessible in the Nile River valley to even the humblest of individuals, making fragrance common and within easy reach throughout the whole of Egypt. It is well known from ancient manuscripts and artwork that the Egyptians were extremely fond of floral garlands, much in the manner of today's Hawaiian lei. There are countless images of lotus flowers being worn and sniffed, however, nowhere does this indigenous flower appear in perfumery recipes. Instead, it seems the Egyptians preferred to use much more luxurious and less common imports such as frankincense, myrrh, cinnamon and cassia for this purpose.

Lotus Flower

The lotus flower has a very long history and even appeared in ancient Egyptian legends. Growing from the mud at the bottom of ponds and streams, the exquisite and pure white or pink flower—with its 15 or more oval, spreading petals—is said to symbolize the sun due to its daily creation and rebirth. The flower rises above the water at dawn to reveal its precious petals before closing again and sinking underwater at night.

Enduring Traditions

ARABIAN STYLE WATER-BASED THERAPIES

Synonymous with Ancient Arabia is bathing. It being sensuous and calming, bathing was used to heal the spirit and treat the body. Egyptians and Babylonians believed that in order to reach a higher spirituality, they had to be clean and beautiful. In pursuit of this coveted position, they practised fumigation to disperse oils, purify the air and provide protection from the evil spirits. They also used oils for healing long before individual herbs were studied for medicinal benefit.

For priests in the service of the gods cleanliness was obligatory; not only did they have to wash several times a day but they had to be clean-shaven all over to keep parasites at bay. Deodorant was much in demand and to further repel body odour, men and women were advised to place little balls of incense and porridge where the limbs met.

Water was plentiful but there is little evidence of the use of natural soaps. Cleansing was accomplished by sitting in a hot bath to open the pores of the skin before oils were expertly massaged into the skin and scraped off, carrying the dirt and impurities with them. Honey and yoghurt were other cleansing favourites with a traditional face mask of yoghurt and honey applied to the skin to deeply exfoliate as lactic acid in the yoghurt helped dissolve the outer skin cells while also brightening the complexion. Honey, served in a therapeutic sense, as a traditional remedy from the Arab world lives to this day—a spoonful of natural honey taken daily to boost immunity or honey mixed with lemon to treat a cough (see pages 62–65).

THIS PAGE: **Arabian style lanterns are used to decorate the spa exterior.**
OPPOSITE: **Milk and yoghurt were cleansing favourites due to their lactic acid content, which dissolves dead skin cells and brightens the complexion.**

THIS PAGE (FROM TOP): Moisturizers and lotions have been used to soften the skin for centuries; the tepidarium in the hammam at One&Only Royal Mirage in Dubai, typically this room is used to prepare the body for the hammam rituals.
OPPOSITE: Inside the main dome-shaped room, bathers rest on the warm marble slab and relax until it's their turn for an all-over body scrub.

Natron Toothpaste

To create a semblance of natron toothpaste at home simply mix a little water with baking soda, stir with a toothbrush before brushing teeth. It's clean, refreshing and effective but if overused the baking soda may eventually damage tooth enamel. A drop of essential oil of myrrh can also be added to the paste.

However, to the Egyptian women in particular, bathing was far more than just cleansing; it enhanced beauty and in a society where women maintained an elevated status, her toilette or bathroom routine became legendary. Like the tales of Queen Cleopatra (69-30 BC), ruler of ancient Egypt bathing in milk to keep her skin beautifully soft and pure to the touch. To this day milk baths are used to improve skin tone and texture, while honey, cream and cocoa butter moisturize and soothe.

Before bathing, the debonair Egyptian woman would wash herself thoroughly with a special cleansing paste, made from water mixed with natron. This is a naturally occurring compound of sodium carbonate and sodium bicarbonate which was also used in toothpaste and became a vital component of the mummification process.

Bathing Rituals

While the Egyptians used thermal baths dating back to 2000 BC it was from the Roman style of bathing that the traditional hammam (Arabic for 'spreader of warmth') emerged. The hammam is the Turkish variant of the steam bath that flourished around 600 AD when the prophet Muhammad encouraged his followers to take such baths. Heat, he believed, enhanced fertility.

Being a place of social gathering and ritual cleansing, hammams were generally located next to a mosque or a souk (marketplace) and played a fundamental role in Ottoman culture. The practice managed to combine the functionality and structural elements of its predecessor, the Roman bath, with the Turkish-Muslim traditions of bathing, ritual cleansing and respect for water.

Like its Roman ancestors, the typical hammam consisted of three interconnecting rooms normally used in a graduating sequence of heat: the sogukluk (meaning cool room), the tepidarium (meaning warm room) and the sicaklik (meaning hot room). The sicaklik was the main large domed room, decorated with small glass windows to let in light, and contained a large central marble slab for bathers to lie on, soak up steam and enjoy scrub massages. The tepidarium was used for preparing the body with soap and water and the sogukluk for relaxation, dressing, indulging in a refreshing drink and where available, taking a quiet siesta in private cubicles. Integral to the whole hammam experience was the tellak or attendant who acted as usher, masseur and bouncer, while also scaring off dijans or phantoms.

Unlike the Roman or Byzantine baths of old, the hammam was not exclusive to men, usually having separate quarters for men and women. Being social centres they became part of daily life, populated in almost every occasion with traditional entertainment (for example, dancing and eating especially in the women's quarters) and ceremonies, such as before weddings or celebrating birth.

A Short History of Baths

Nowhere was bathing more a social activity than in the Roman thermae (from the Greek word therme for heat). These baths were surrounded by sports stadiums, gymnasiums, theatres, halls, libraries and inns, with the largest known to accommodate up to 6,000 people at one time. While Emperor Agrippa is credited with building the first Roman thermae in 25 BC, Romans were already using various forms of humbler baths called balnea two centuries before. Every emperor after Agrippa would try to outshine the one before by building more extravagant thermae than his predecessor, thereby leading the way for the baths to become an integral part of life in towns within the empire. They typically comprised a series of chambers and pools of varying temperatures, depending on where they were situated in relation to the heating furnace. The bather would wander between rooms, starting from the coolest and moving to the hottest before completing their ritual in the cold plunge pool.

The Dead Sea

The mineral-rich waters of Israel's Dead Sea are legendary. A geological phenomenon created some 3 million years ago during a great natural upheaval in which layers of mineral-rich earth were exposed and salt springs erupted, forming a valley containing a closed lake 400 metres (1,300 feet) below sea level. Thousands of years of evaporation increased the levels of salts and minerals in the lake, known today as the Dead Sea. With a salt concentration of up to 33 per cent (compared with about three per cent in the Mediterranean), at least 21 different minerals and trace elements including calcium, chloride, iodine, copper, magnesium, radium and zinc (half of which are found in no other sea or ocean) and a unique concentration of biological muds, it is one of nature's richest sources of minerals. This uniquely powerful blend is excellent for skin conditions such as acne, psoriasis and eczema while also improving cell metabolism and detoxification. But it's the complete weightlessness experienced when floating on the Dead Sea that it is best known for, along with its rejuvenation and rehabilitation benefits. Since the time of Aristotle (304–322 BC), who is credited as saying that 'very bitter and salty water in which no fish can live and where neither man nor animal can sink,' people have come to the region to experience its healing waters and enjoy its natural beauty.

THIS PAGE: **A lady of the desert, a Bedouin woman with her elaborate costume.**
OPPOSITE (FROM TOP): **Across the Middle East, spas draw upon the healing waters of the Dead Sea, while floating in a salt-water pool, the body absorbs the rich minerals and nutrients; clusters of salt in the Dead Sea.**

The Bedouin People

Bedouin, an Arabic word meaning 'desert dweller', best describes the small, tightly-knit tribes of nomadic people who were the largest and primary inhabitants of the vast expanse of desert that was ancient Arabia. The majority of Bedouin are Arabic-speaking Muslims and to this day they constitute a small minority of the population of the Middle East and North Africa living across a wide area of land.

As few places in the desert could support the life of even a small community for an extended period of time, the Bedouin clustered in tribes, leading a life of continuous mobility. They lived in tents and stayed on the move in search of water and what meagre pasture the parched land afforded their flocks. Making use of the desert, the Bedouin tribe still uses traditional healing methods.

Tribes were usually headed by a chieftain or shayak, a position that was proudly handed down from father to eldest son. People were divided into social classes depending on ancestry and profession. Passing from one class to another was relatively feasible, but marriage between a man and woman of different classes was not.

The various Bedouin tribes had no central authority to bring them together and organize their lives. There was, however, a common social structure: the tribal system, where there was allegiance to the tribe and a code of honour, to which they strictly adhered to. Unruly and undisciplined by nature, the Bedouin was happy to be 'his own king' as long as he abided by the unwritten laws of the tribe. The Bedouin grazed his flock and often joined other members of the tribe in raiding other tribes and trade caravans, an activity which had developed as a way of life for most desert dwellers. Content with this mode of existence, the Bedouin was generally unaware of the civilization which existed at the threshold of his habitat.

A typical Bedouin tent was made of goat or camel hair or plant fibres and was customarily divided into two sections by a woven curtain known as a ma'nad. One section, reserved for men and the reception of most guests, is called the majlis, or 'sitting place.' The other, in which the women cook and receive female guests, is called the maharama, or 'place of the women.'

A shared respect for the dangers and hardship of desert life imbued Bedouin culture with a celebrated sense of hospitality, the latter of which is a common trait among Arabic people across the Middle East. In the vast silence and brooding solitude of the desert's open space, simply encountering another person was, and in some regions still is, an unusual and noteworthy event. A new face was a cause for great interest, generosity and common civility, all values celebrated in traditional poetry and songs.

The traditions still exist today, and if lucky enough to visit a Bedouin tent, guests are welcomed, honoured, respected and nourished with copious amounts of deliciously fresh, cardamom-spiced coffee. The Bedouin host must follow strict traditions and guidelines when entertaining guests. For example, there are three expressions for pouring coffee when greeting honoured guests:
El-Heif This is spoken when the first cup of cardamom coffee is poured. This cup is initially tasted by the Bedouin host to make sure the guests feel completely safe and welcome.

women which helped thicken and strengthen hair, and protect it from sun damage. For those who could afford the luxury, coconut oil was widely used for thick hair. Also, olive oil was applied warm to treat a flaky scalp. A red mud called arjeel, traditionally bought from Iran or Oman, was the Bedouin shampoo of choice.

Dairy products, milk and meat comprised the bulk of the traditional Bedouin diet. The traditional meal, or mensaf, is rice covered with meat (beef or lamb) and cooked with yoghurt.

Bedouin tribes made their graves by simply placing a stone at the head of the grave and one at its foot. Moreover it was traditional to leave the clothes of the deceased on top of the grave to be adopted by needy travellers passing by.

El-Keif These words are uttered when the second cup of coffee is poured and tasted by the guest.
El-Dheif This is said when the third cup of coffee is served. This cup is to be poured and drunk by the guest himself.

Traditionally, visitors were cause for great celebration which was done with music, poetry and dance. The traditional instruments of Bedouin musicians are the shabbaba, a length of metal fashioned into a type of flute, the rababa, a versatile single-string violin and of course, the voice. Women are the main singers and they sit in rows facing each other as they exchange commentary by song.

Without the material wealth, cosmetics were scant and simple. Creams and oils served the dual purpose of beautification and medicine. For example, henna was the major beauty herb for both men and

Traditional Bedouin Dress

Whether in the teeming cities or solitary plains, women traditionally wear a long, black, hooded robe called a jalabiyya, that is intricately embroidered with deep winged sleeves. The square block of dense embroidery on the bodice holds outstanding workmanship and colour. A married woman will generally have red as the predominant colour, while blue is reserved for unmarried girls and widows. All women are required to keep their hair covered. Married women wrap a black cloth known as asaba about their forehead, while the head and face of the unmarried woman is protected by a bourque. Bedouin ladies love to lavish themselves with expensive jewellery and exotic fragrances.

Men traditionally wear a head cloth called a kufiyya, which is secured with a rope called an agal. The head rope in particular carries great significance, being indicative of the wearer's ability to uphold the obligations and responsibilities of manhood.

THIS PAGE: **Drinking coffee with a Bedouin tribe is a momentous occasion.**
OPPOSITE: **The dramatic Arabian desert is a stark but beautiful home.**

A Purely Arabian Indulgence

TRADITIONS OF OPULENCE

With its deeply embedded history of the ancient Hakims and Cleopatra and today's modern opulence, Arabia offers a fascinating and eclectic mix of ancient and modern, East and West. Futuristic architecture, garish hotels, designer shopping malls constantly pushing the frontiers of luxury, go hand-in-hand with the unchanging calm of the stark, open desert just minutes away, home to the Bedouin, his camels and falcons, oryx and gazelle bounding over endless sand dunes.

The Arabian Peninsula stretches from the Sahara desert down to the United Arab Emirates; it encompasses the dramatic scenery of the Hajar Mountains and the Aladdin's cave of cultural delights and fabulously remote beaches of the Omani coast. In Dubai, first impressions are breathtaking with indisputably spectacular hotels and spas. As befits the only seven-star hotel in the world, the Burj Al Arab is the most exciting, opulent and outrageously over-the-top experience one could possibly imagine—flaming torches and fountains shooting magnificent columns of water, set the scene for the blatantly lavish drama of the sumptuous gold and red interiors complete with waterfalls spilling dry ice and glass-encased coral reefs leading to the tallest atrium in the world.

Less than one hour's drive from Dubai lies the idyllic oasis of Al Maha hidden among the red sands of the desert. If sand-boarding, 'dune-bashing' in 4x4 vehicles, eco-safaris, camel rides or simply soaking up the serenity of the desert under a canopy of stars is on the agenda, then—in this land of contrasts—the desert is the place. One cannot help but marvel at its quiet grandeur, the early morning glimpse of the desert sunrise, unsurpassed views, towering sand dunes and imposingly vast landscapes. Feel the rush of the wind while speeding down the slopes of the sand dunes, or peacefully observing desert gazelles and camels wandering through the remote expanse of rolling dunes and desert savannah. The magic that is the Arabian Desert sunset, a bonfire under a starlit sky, is the perfect end to a day in paradise.

THIS PAGE: **A suite at the Chedi Muscat, simplistic style in a truly luxurious spa.**
OPPOSITE: **Style and splendour at the Six Senses Spa at Madinat Jumeirah, where guests can relax in any of a number of grand majlis.**

A spa break in the Near East is not just about escaping to fabulous hotels and spas in the winter sun. Seductive as they are, there is far more to the land of the Pharaohs and its Levantine sisters (encompassing Jordan, Lebanon and Syria) that makes them a fascinating blend of ancient marvels and modern comforts with a near perfect climate. One cannot fail to be completely overawed by the sheer magnitude of the mighty monuments of Cairo,

THIS PAGE (FROM TOP): An example of Arabia's spa opulence is the room amenities, at Al Maha, Bulgari products are supplied in all the guest rooms, ensuring hair and body are luxuriously cared for; the signature treatment at Six Senses offers a purely indulgent spa treatment.
OPPOSITE: Dubai's desert offers space and calm, ensuring five-star pampering.

the Pyramids of Giza and the inscrutable Sphinx in the realization that Egypt was once the cradle of one of the world's most powerful civilizations. Contemplate cruising the River Nile, quietly drifting from temple to exquisite temple before decamping at yet another exotic and magical resort on the shores of the Red Sea where the mountains and desert of the Sinai give way to waters offering possibly the best scuba-diving and snorkelling

opportunities in the world. In this land of astounding contrasts, this is eminently possible.

Built in splendour, many of Arabia's spas offer the opulence of ancient Egypt and Babylon with up-to-the-minute therapies taking you on a journey where everything you see, smell, hear, taste and touch, enhances the senses, creating a feeling of pure ecstasy. Some portray the hallmarks of the Bedouin with hand-woven carpets, rich brocades and Arabian antiques while others are lavishly opulent, exuding gold and precious gems as befits

Tale of Velvet Nights

What better way to enjoy spa indulgence Arabian-style than by reliving the legacy of the Tale of Velvet Nights. This royal treatment, inspired by ancient tales of love and passion, is set amid the stark but opulent beauty of Arabia and based on the ancient recipe that was part of secret harem rituals before the young woman was presented to the Sultan. Arabian incense burns and delicate rose petals float on a scented bath in preparation for the princess who enters the room escorted by her flock of handmaidens. After stepping into the glistening water she is thoroughly massaged. As she is helped from the bath, smoke from incense gathered from desert trees purifies her body in preparation for the gentle kneading with an ancient recipe of nuts, fruits, flowers and oils to exfoliate and nourish the skin. When the skin is as smooth and polished as the silks she will wear, exotic hot perfumed oils are applied to soothe and calm the senses before unqualified relaxation in the palace she calls home.

the modern Arabian experience. Regardless of design, all spas are warm, friendly and pampering with exotic aromas wafting through and deeply indulgent rituals designed to soothe the body and make the spirit soar.

Relive the legend of Cleopatra with ancient milk bath rituals and the modern take on the hammam and rasul. Combine these with decadent precious stone and crushed pearl treatments, aromatherapy and first-class facials or tap into the body's innate healing with massages using coloured gem stones—try rose quartz for compassion, emerald for love,

prosperity and pleasant dreams, amethyst for spirituality and diamond for physical rejuvenation and spiritual uplift.

Then there is the quintessential flower of Arabia, the most elegant and delicate of them all, the rose in all its guises—rose steam, rosewater and incense, Rose of Damascus Luxury Body Polish, and Rose Milk Bath. The subject of countless books and legends, much loved aphrodisiac and purifier of the mosque in ancient Persia, where else could one experience the purity and goodness of this enduring flower but in its Arabian home.

Arabian Spa Therapies

ANCIENT AND MODERN COMBINE

Ancient infuses with the contemporary in the modern Arabian experience in spas throughout the Gulf and beyond. From bathing Cleopatra-style to the use of hammams, rasuls and 1,000-year-old crystals and precious gems, the Arabian spa today has taken on more of a pampering rather than therapeutic role. Designed in opulence and sheer luxury, spas in the Middle East are reinventing these ancient therapies and enhancing their benefits by combining them with more modern rejuvenating and revitalizing rituals. From classic cures with indigenous ingredients such as henna, honey, dates, saffron and the eternally enduring rose, to more sophisticated rituals based on precious stones and crystals, these ancient rituals have been reborn and, with the lavishness that is the Arabian spa, you can taste, touch and feel the difference.

THIS PAGE: Reiki, a Japanese touch therapy that channels energy to replenish and re-balance, is practised in Arabia's modern and spas.
OPPOSITE: Drawing from the Hawaiian hot stone treatment, desert stones are used.

Water-Based Therapy

As research is increasingly recognizing the physical, psychological and rehabilitative benefits of water-based therapies, ancient holistic bathing rituals have been reinvented and adopted in the contemporary Arabian spa. A relaxing soak in a deep, hot bath is considered essential to well-being as the goodness of the heat and scented waters are easily absorbed through the skin, purifying and enriching every vessel in the body.

Whether it's bathing in the mineral-rich waters of the Dead Sea or bringing a taste of this to the home in the increasing number of commercial products, encapsulating the Dead Sea goodness is easier than ever and what's more, it's extremely good for the skin.

The Hammam

While the original hammam concept (see pages 30–31) is thriving in the modern spa, the overall style is somewhat different. The contemporary experience takes place in a fully tiled chamber with walls, floor and lounge benches steam-heated to a temperature

of between 60°C–80°C (140°F–176°F). The aromatic moist atmosphere and automatic dispersion of aromatherapy essences (most commonly eucalyptus) helps stimulate blood circulation as the body gradually heats, which then initiates a natural process of purifying and cleansing.

In ancient times, special accessories for women were on hand, some of which are still in use today, such as the pestemal (a special cloth of silk and/or cotton that covers the body, like a pareos), nalin (special wooden clogs—often decorated with silver or mother-of-pearl—which prevent the wearer from slipping on the wet floor), a kehsa or rough mitt for massage, along with accessories such as gilded soap boxes, embroidered mirrors, jewel boxes, henna bowls and perfume bottles.

After about 20 minutes the body is rinsed with a Kneipp cool water hose to refresh and further stimulate circulation. The client then rests and replaces lost water. The modern hammam is generally part of an overall ritual combining bathing with massage, scrubs or even facial treatments. The Shiffa Hammam Ancienne experience at Six Senses Spa at Madinat Jumeirah in Dubai, for example, is based on the ancient hammam ritual. This experience goes one step further including nutrient-rich clay exfoliation, perfumed waters, heated stones and sand to leave the body feeling completely clean and energized. A facial hammam treatment is also available as is a hair and body mask.

The Rasul

Rasul is a traditional Arabian cleansing ritual that is administered in an elaborately tiled steam chamber that has a domed starlight ceiling. An aromatic steam injector softly infuses a mixture of dried herbs to help cleanse and detoxify.

After taking a short shower, medicinal muds (such as Dead Sea mud) are applied to specific areas of the body to cleanse and exfoliate. The mud is gently massaged before it hardens. As the humidity of the rasul increases, the mud gradually liquefies and a slight prickly feeling may be experienced. After approximately 20 minutes of heat,

THIS PAGE: A modern hammam ritual involves an all-over body treatment, with a scrub, massage and sometimes even a facial and hair mask.
OPPOSITE (FROM TOP): A hammam tellak, the masseur and guard of the baths; bathers wash themselves first before the tellak scrubs the body with a pesternal.

THIS PAGE (FROM TOP): Mud is applied to the face to absorb oils and detoxify the skin; varying in consistency and colour muds should be mixed for specific skin types.
OPPOSITE: The Dead Sea's mineral-rich mud that is rubbed directly onto the skin.

Dead Sea Mud Wrap

Initially developed to ease joint pain, inflammation and swelling, the Dead Sea Mud Wrap is increasingly used in spas to cleanse and rejuvenate. The mud's ability to flush toxins and excess fluid makes it a very useful treatment for lower back pain and pre-menstrual bloating while its mineral-rich Dead Sea black mud is a legendary therapy for skin problems such as acne, eczema and psoriasis.

Moor Mud Wrap

Moor is a rich accumulation of water-logged plant deposits including roots, flowers, fruits and seeds. Moor mud is believed to contain anti-inflammatory and astringent properties that are ideal detoxifying agents. The healing properties, also make the mud suitable for treating arthritic conditions, hormonal and fertility problems and skin issues such as acne, eczema and psoriasis. To create a healing bath, the moor is mixed well in warm water to prevent it from sticking together. Essential oils can also be added before soaking for up to 30 minutes for maximum benefit. The bath can be enjoyed in a tub with jets or with an underwater hose to massage specific body parts.

Pelotherapy

Technically referred to as peloids (from the Greek pelos for mud), mud comprises about one-third earth and two-thirds water. In the spa context, the term generally means substances that come from mineral-rich areas around natural springs, moors, volcanoes and waters such as the Dead Sea. Muds have exfoliating properties, they increase circulation and aid the removal of waste products.

Pelotherapy, or the use of mud for medicinal purposes, features mud packs, wraps or baths that, as according to the Greek physician Galen, can be used to treat ailments such as rheumatic and arthritic pain, inflammatory diseases and skin and digestive complaints.

As mud is water-soluble it helps the skin absorb its indigenous nutrients and despite its association with dirt, the skin will tingle with cleanliness.

a tropical warm rain shower falls from the dome of the rasul to gently wash away the mud, leaving the skin silky smooth and revitalized. Relaxing beneath a canopy of a 1,000 star-lights and the powerful cleansing effects are soon felt on the skin and respiratory system.

Although traditionally a ritual in itself, as part of the modern spa experience rasul is generally used before a massage or other treatments (such as Cleopatra's milk bath) to gently ease physical and emotional tension.

Crystal and Gem Therapy

Mythology and history abound with accounts of stones being used in a myriad of ways from healing common ailments to bestowing status, luck and health on their owners. In the lavishness of today's Arabian spa these rich and precious gems are truly at home in the opulent surrounds and therapeutic rituals created based on the powerful benefits these gems possess.

Crystals bridge the gap between science and magic; as silicon chips they are used to receive, store and transmit information in computers, radio and telecommunications. In exactly the same way they are used in healing and meditation—to receive, store and transmit energy. Crystals are grounding. It has long been believed that we are more than the matter of our physical bodies; we have an energy body that vibrates at will each time we release a thought, and crystals help attune us to this energy from the magnetic core of the earth from where they came thousands of years ago.

In healing, crystals are believed to transmit and receive energy, thereby restoring balance and amplifying our innate healing ability. They have extremely high and exact rates of vibration which can be precisely manipulated and used to modify thoughts, emotions and the energy fields of human bodies. For those who take the time to consciously attune to the energy of crystals, by working with them a whole new world will open as they begin to feel the Earth as a living spirit.

Practitioners learn to tap into the crystals' unique energy, thereby enhancing the healing of emotional or physical complaints. The practitioner may hold the crystal in one hand, resting the other on the affected part of the body, while asking the person to visualize the energy that is channelling through the crystal. Alternatively the crystal may be placed on specific acupuncture points along the body to facilitate interaction with innate electromagnetic energy. Alternatively, the person might be given a crystal to wear as a bracelet or to place in their room.

Crystal therapy is often performed in conjunction with reiki and colour therapy (see

Crystal Clearing

Crystals are said to contain a healing life energy that can be charged or discharged like a battery. They are thought to respond to all kinds of vibrations from the environment and from those who come in contact with them. Besides 'clearing' new crystals before use, it is essential to clear them regularly to rid them of this jumbled energy. It is also important to clear second-hand jewellery of the former owners' energy for at least one week before wearing it. As clearing methods differ for different crystals it is best to seek expert advice before clearing. Some of the more common crystal clearing methods include:

- Leaving crystals outdoors during a full moon.
- Soaking crystals in a bowl of spring water with a pinch of sea salt.
- Exposing crystals to the sun for one hour.
- Burying crystals under sand for a few hours.
- Standing crystals in a running brook.
- 'Smudging' crystals by wafting them with smoking herbs like sage or sweet grass.

THIS PAGE (FROM TOP): Placing a crystal on the third eye and around the body will encourage energy flow and clear the mind, the crystal can also be used to recall dreams or to help receive a guiding dream about a specific subject.

OPPOSITE: Crystals can be placed around the room to store and transmit energy.

page 50). It may also be used in absent healing when a practitioner endeavours to form an intuitive link with someone not in the same physical space by projecting energies from the crystal to the person in need of healing. In all cases, visualization is the ultimate key to success, as both the healer and recipient visualize balance and ease of flow. The healer becomes simply the channel for pure positive energy as stagnant energy melts away and new vitality fills the energy field.

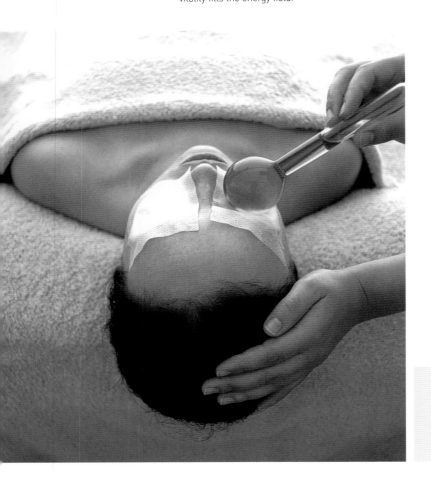

The Aura

Practitioners who work with auras believe that all living things have an electromagnetic field, body of energy or aura that forms an oval shape around the body. Yale University's neuroanatomist Professor Harold Saxton Burr was the first to measure this energy field in the 1930s, calling it the L-field or 'life field' and many psychics or energy healers claim to perceive its emanations intuitively. Others use biofeedback sensors, computers and photographic devices to record and analyse these fields.

A person's aura characteristics are believed to change with illness, moods or the environment and can be a reflection of their physical, psychological and spiritual well-being. The more spiritually healthy, the larger and brighter the aura. For those with low energy levels, their aura will appear smaller and duller than normal. Auras are thought to extend 5–8 centimetres (2–3 inches) around the body and have seven layered bands, each reflecting different facets of personality corresponding in colour with each of the chakras or energy centres. The etheric sheath—the band nearest the body—draws life force from the atmosphere and distributes it through the chakras in the body (see below).

Chakras

In the etheric body, each of the chakras represents a series of seven centres of electromagnetic energy that are located along the course of the spine which can help further explain how the body's energy is intimately linked to the earth. Chakras (a Sanskrit word meaning wheel) have no physical form, yet directly influence specific glands and functions within the physical body.

Each chakra vibrates at a different rate and spins in a different direction depending on whether it is absorbing or releasing energy. Each has a particular colour and function assigned to it. For example, the base chakra, found at the base of the spine, is ruby red in colour and is linked to the basic instincts of survival—food, clothes, shelter and rest. Here, at the base of the spine, lies the kundalini energy, the sexual energy and basic instinct to procreate. The chakras are linked by nadis, through which energy flows around the body.

All chakras are equally important and must be kept clear and open for inner peace and well-being. Healthy, free-flowing and grounding lower chakras are a prerequisite for maximizing the inspirations; visions and creative energy emanate from the higher chakras. Any imbalance in the body should be treated with the relevant colour and a simple crystal healing practice is to place crystals of the appropriate colour and energy at corresponding chakra points (see chart below). This is believed to cleanse and renew the chakras, leaving you feeling more focused and energized.

Chakra	Location	Colour	Stone	Governs
Base	base of spine	ruby red	garnet, ruby, onyx	basic survival, connection to Earth
Belly/Sacral	just below naval	warm/vibrant orange	hematite, moonstone	sensuality and sexuality, guides emotions
Solar Plexus	mid abdomen	bright/sunny yellow	citrine, topaz	self-worth, stores and distributes body's energy
Heart	mid chest	emerald green/rose pink	rose quartz	love and compassion
Throat	throat	bright blue	aquamarine	communication and self expression
Third Eye	between eyes	deep indigo blue	sapphire, amethyst	insight and intuition
Crown	above top of head	deep amethyst	clear quartz, amethyst	inspiration, enlightenment, cosmic consciousness

THIS PAGE: Different coloured stones or crystals can be placed along the chakra points to unblock the flow of energy.
OPPOSITE: Another modern innovation in Arabia's opulent spas is the La Prairie Eye Bliss Treatment available at the Assawan Spa, Burj Al Arab.

Colour Therapy

Colour is light vibrating at different rates and, to those working with it, a powerful healing force. Each colour emits its own subtle energy vibration that affects the body's chakras and associated stones. For example, red stones such as ruby and garnet relate to the base chakra and are used for calming and grounding the central nervous system, while amethyst or violet stones such as quartz and amethyst, that are associated with the crown, open the connection to the cosmic world, encouraging the wearer to surrender to the higher power.

In the world of spa, crystals and gems are increasingly being used as vehicles for energy transfer in massage oils and specific therapies. In massage, the gem energizes by transferring its energy to the oil which, when massaged onto the skin, activates and re-balances the receiver's innate energy. Even by wearing them as jewellery or placing them (on their own or as a gem tincture) in a glass of water overnight and drinking it the next day, the positive effects of the gem can be experienced. When gems are used for healing they must first be purified by immersing them in salted water (or sacred waters like the Ganges in India) for at least two days.

Experts believe that the virtue of gemstones lies in their tints, their reflectivity and their energies which will differ depending on whether the gem is polished, cut or in its natural state. For example, the Dubai-based skincare company Shiffa best exemplifies how precious stones can be used in the spa experience. Shiffa places its precious gems in bottles of massage oil blends specifically chosen for their harmony with the particular gemstone. Some ingredients in the oil share an affinity with the gem while others are chosen for their affinity with the gem's colour and properties. For example the essential oils of attar of rose, myrtle, neroli, and the oils of macadamia, camilla, and evening primrose all share an affinity with diamond and feature in Shiffa's Diamond Body Gem Massage Oil.

When laying on hands during colour therapy, the healer should place the right hand on the solar plexus of the recipient and the left over the problem area, the healer should then visualize the colour that is needed and imagine it flowing down the right arm into and around the recipient's nervous system, before completing the circuit at the left hand.

Coloured light healing, also known as chromatherapy, uses light that can either be diffused over the whole body or just a specific problem area. It's believed that different coloured lights travel at different frequencies; for example, violet radiates in short waves and soothes the emotions, red radiates in long waves and energizes the body. In the home, candles and light filters can be used.

THIS PAGE: **During treatment, energy is channelled through the healer's hands who uses visualization, which is crucial to the whole healing process.**
OPPOSITE: **A colour therapy room where lights alternate in colour while the therapist uses the hands to heal the body.**

Some Commonly Used Gems

Gold This precious metal is lavishly used in present-day Arabia with hotels such as the Burj Al Arab in Dubai sprinkling gold on food for its valued guests.

Gold has been used for centuries, it may even be the first metal ever used by man, and its number of healing myths has added to its preciousness. The mysticism surrounding the metal has given rise to a human lust for gold, which in turn has undoubtedly amplified the powers attributed to it. So much so that many new age healers call gold 'the master healer'. This comes as little surprise considering the desire that gold has incurred throughout history has approached something almost like worship.

In healing, gold symbolizes purity of spirit with healers attributing the powers of cell regeneration, energy conductivity, communication transmission and energy purification to the metal. In healing it is believed that gold spurs the regeneration of neurotransmitters in both lobes of the brain, creating a balance of brain function between creative and logical thought. Also with its ability to improve information flow through the body, it is believed to have beneficial effects on the nervous system.

In the world of spiritual healing, gold is believed to have the emotional power to ease tension, feelings of inferiority and anger as well as encouraging the realization of one's innate potential. On a physical level, gold's lack of toxicity combined with its incredible malleability, strength as an energy conductor and resistance to wear and corrosion, make it a highly useful resourse in science. Its medical uses have included the treatment of arthritis and dental fixtures and certain blood, skin and neurological disorders. Some healers believe gold to

be such a powerful energy generator and remover of blockages that it has been used to strengthen, amplify and conduct energy in the treatment of autism, dyslexia, epilepsy and scoliosis

Diamond In both myth and in gem therapy, diamonds are associated with harmony and higher spiritual attainment. They are said to help remove blockages and negativity and to promote mental clarity. Diamonds, although clear, can absorb all colours and these can be seen when light is reflected onto the gem.

The Shiffa Diamond Body Gem Massage Oil comprises diamond blended with the essential oils of attar of rose, myrtle, neroli, and the oils of camilla, macadamia, and evening primrose. It is used to re-balance those suffering from physical or emotional imbalance, workaholics, as well as those with stressed skin, stretch marks and scarring.

Emerald The emerald represents stability and strength. Described as a subtle gem, it is used as a symbol of love, prosperity, and goodness, as well as to balance the heart and promote pleasant dreams. Emeralds are found in varying shades of green depending upon where they are mined.

The Shiffa Emerald Body Gem Massage Oil contains added essential oils of vetiver, cedarwood, nard, juniper and the oils of peach, macadamia, jojoba and evening primrose and is best used to promote physical and emotional strength, tranquillity and for meditation. In facial therapy, emerald is an excellent skin balancer for dry, greyish or combination skins.

Ruby The ruby represents stimulation, vitality, passion and happiness while also promoting tranquillity, increased intuition and assisting in overall well-being. Rubies vary in shades of red from the very dark to light red, with the colour depending on the location of the mine and the minerals that have been absorbed by the gem.

The Shiffa Ruby Body Gem Massage Oil encompasses some of the most precious essential oils such as three types of attar of rose and an intricate blend of 12 essential oils including sesame, jojoba, evening primrose and peach, each chosen for its vitamin content and therapeutic value. The ruby-infused oil is used to combat stress, premature skin ageing, muscular problems, stretch marks and cellulite while also energizing tired and lifeless skin.

Sapphire These precious gems come in many colours from deep blues to pink with the blue sapphire having the shortest wave length and therefore best used for sensitive, distressed, sun-exposed and blemished skin types. Sapphires represent peace, devotion, clarity, inspiration and spiritual awareness and help cool and calm physical and emotional disharmony.

Shiffa's Sapphire Body Gem Massage Oil is a blend of neroli, camomile, clary sage and mandarin as well as the oils of macadamia, sesame and sweet almond, which combine with sapphire to produce a gentle and sensitive massage oil with an affinity for the healing properties of this precious gem.

THIS PAGE (FROM TOP): Shiffa's precious ingredients; flakes of gold float in the Shiffa body spray, where the healing properties are infused directly into the oil. OPPOSITE: Gold is seen as 'the master healer' and is used to aid the nervous system, and even brain function.

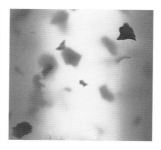

- Mixing aloe vera with a vitamin E capsule. To make lotion, simply pierce the capsule to release the vitamin E and mix with aloe vera gel. Apply generously onto the sunburnt skin.

Sunburn Therapies

While the sun gives life to the earth, provides warmth and keeps us energized, it is also the primary cause of wrinkles, saggy, sunken skin and skin cancer on overexposed skin.

As the Arabian sun is consistently powerful and damaging, soothing after-sun therapies are a highlight in Middle Eastern spas; for example, the Sunburn Soother signature therapy at the Six Senses in the Madinat Jumeirah, Dubai. This treatment combines aloe vera therapy, to moisturize and encourage new cell growth, with foot acupressure and a scalp massage. At Al Maha Desert Resort & Spa, a pre-sun treatment sees the skin exfoliated before protective sun lotion is applied. At the Hyatt Regency in Sharm El Sheikh, a cooling aloe vera wrap is adminstered to soothe sun-kissed skin. Other after-sun measures at home include:

- A cool shower or bath and placing cold, wet cloths, that have been infused with lavender, on the burn.
- Wiping thinly sliced cucumber in a circular motion over the affected areas.
- Drinking plenty of water to counteract the drying effects from the sun.
- Diluting apple cider vinegar with equal parts water, using a spray bottle and misting the skin to help prevent blistering and peeling.

Sunburn is better prevented than treated. Effective sunscreens are available in a wide variety of strengths. Most doctors recommend a generous application of sunscreen with an SPF level of 30 or greater. If you are out in the sun for a prolonged period of time during the day, wearing a hat and other protective clothing is highly recommended. Light clothing is recommended as it reflects the sun most effectively.

Aloe Vera Sunburn Spray
20 drops lavender oil
20 drops tea tree oil
20 drops camomile oil
100 ml (3½ fl oz/½ cup) aloe vera juice
Mix aloe vera and oils together, pour into a spray bottle. Shake well before spraying the affected area several times a day.

Aloe Vera & Honey Sunburn Spray
¼ cup dried calendula flowers
¼ cup dried lavender buds
¼ cup peppermint
85 ml (3 fl oz/¼ cup) honey
425 ml (15 fl oz/2 cups) water
Place water in a pan. Bring to a boil, reduce heat and add herbs. Leave on a low heat for 10–15 minutes. Strain and add aloe vera juice and honey. Mix well. Pour mixture into a spray bottle and spray affected area several times a day.

THIS PAGE: **Massaging aloe vera into sun-kissed skin will help to ease any sunburn.**
OPPOSITE: **The Middle East, with its vast deserts and sun-drenched shores, calls for a stronger sunscreen and more caution in the unrelenting sun.**

Arabian Spa Products

NATURAL GOODNESS OF THE MIDDLE EAST

The Middle East proffers a multitude of naturally grown products covering an array of nutritional benefits for the body both outside and within. Spas across Arabia are using time-honoured traditions such as the art of henna, which has lived on and spread around the world. Traditionally used to cool the body in the desert heat, it's common for people to decorate their hands and feet with elaborate henna designs and to use it to strengthen and protect their hair. Milk and honey evoke visions of Cleopatra languishing in her bronze bath. Still common today, spas offer milk baths on the menu to soften the skin and honey is a common ingredient in facial treatments. An early indication of Arabia's opulence is the production of saffron. More expensive in weight than gold, the spice can be mixed with sandalwood to create an exotic fragrance.

Fruit has played an important role in the Arabian diet for centuries. From early times, the influence of food has been recognized as a potential basis of cures from diseases. Dates have always been treasured as a highly nutritious food source and are valued for their medicinal benefits.

Over the following pages, each Arabian spa product is considered in detail and handy recipes enable a luxury Arabian experience at home.

THIS PAGE: Different herbs and spices that can be used to make up body treatments such as exfoliating scrubs and skin soothing wraps.
OPPOSITE: Dates can be mixed to make up an enriching moisturizer.

Henna

Henna (lawsonia alba) is a dwarf shrub 2.5–3 metres (8–10 feet) high with small white and yellow, sweet-smelling flowers that, in ancient times, grew primarily in Egypt and Syria. Archaeological research indicates that henna was used by the Pharaohs to stain fingernails and toes prior to mummification, while many medieval paintings depicted the Queen of Sheba decorated with henna on her journey to meet Solomon. Henna's powdered leaves have been used in the Middle East, India and Africa for centuries for dying hair, body and nails and treating a myriad of medicinal complaints.

Traditionally used on the hair, hands and feet of both men and women, henna thickened, strengthened and cooled the head and was used on the body for tattooing and as a sunscreen. The art of applying henna varied tremendously between cultures with different designs having diverse meanings from good health, fertility and wisdom to spiritual enlightenment. Arabic henna designs are usually large, floral patterns on the hands and feet while in India, henna is painted in fine lines for lacy, floral and paisley patterns that cover entire hands, forearms, feet and shins. Intricate henna patterns are obligatory for weddings and other celebrations and a common sight on wealthier women of the tribe. The natural henna pigment penetrates the skin and lasts for several weeks.

Henna's healing powers are legendary with myths depicting the seeds of the plant being powdered and mixed with ghee and made into small pellets which were swallowed with water to cure dysentery. Concoctions were prepared from the bark of the plant to prevent jaundice and enlargement of the liver. Also, the pain and discomfort of a sore throat was relieved by gargling with a decoction made from henna leaves, while sun-induced headaches were relieved by a plaster of henna flowers in vinegar which was applied to the forehead. To control dandruff, henna was mixed with lemon juice and yoghurt. To promote a luxuriant growth of new hair, the leaves are added to boiling oil and massaged into the scalp when cool. Applied directly on the skin henna leaves helped relieve problems such as boils, burns, prickly heat as well as rheumatic conditions, inflammatory swellings, bruises and leprosy.

Henna Skin Balm
Lawsonia in henna serves as an antiseptic skin balm and does not stain the skin.
2–3 tbsp neutral uncolored henna powder
130 ml (4 fl oz/½ cup) warm apple cider vinegar
Mix henna powder with warm vinegar to form a paste. Apply directly to the affected area of the skin.

Henna Scalp Treatment
A more modern use of henna for reducing hair loss.
1 tbsp henna flower oil
1 tbsp jojoba extract
1 tbsp calendula infused oil
½ tsp carrot seed oil
2 drops essential oil of clove
4 drops essential oil of rosemary
5 drops essential oil of patchouli
2 drops essential oil of cedarwood
Combine all ingredients in a bottle and shake well. The bottle should be warmed before massaging a few drops into the scalp before bedtime. Apply 2–3 times per week for best results.

THIS PAGE: The intricate patterns are painted onto the hands, feet and sometimes the forearms and shins.
OPPOSITE: Henna leaves are dried and ground to a powder and mixed with eucalyptus oil and lemon juice to form a paste, when applied to the skin the temporary tattoo will last for several days.

Dates

Called the 'tree of life', according to Muslim legend, the date palm was made from the dust left over from the creation of Adam. Probably the first farmed tree in history, it has grown in the Levant for at least 8,000 years. There are directions for the date palm's cultivation recorded on some 5,000-year-old sun-baked bricks from Mesopotamia. The palm originated in China and was exported to Iran. In the 17th century, pioneering Spaniards brought the seeds to California. Today about three quarters of the world's date crop is grown in the Middle East where it continues to be a prized delicacy.

The date palm is so intrinsically linked with Arabian culture that it has become a treasured food source and is widely used for its medicinal qualities. In 5,000 BC, the Babylonians fermented the fruit of date palms to create a date vinegar that was used for disinfecting insect and snake bites. Bedouin people traditionally use dates, most likely combined with honey, as an antiseptic to aid the healing of wounds, while it is customary for women to eat dates prior to childbirth as the plant is believed to relax the mother, ease muscle pain and reduce bleeding.

Date Treatments

Dates can be used to protect the skin due to the regenerating and anti-ageing properties that help reduce fine lines and improve skin barrier function. The following simple date recipes can easily be prepared at home:

Date Face Cream To make this lotion, extract the seeds of the finest quality dates available and separate the fruit from the skin. Place the fruit in a bowl and mix with a favourite moisturizer. Apply as regular face cream.

Cooling Golden Gel with Dates Combine date extract, peach extract, honey and incense with a cooling body gel and apply to the skin for a regenerating gel that will soothe skin irritations.

Date Body Lotion Blend a favourite body lotion with some date extract, a vitamin B capsule, honey, cocoa-butter, apricot kernel oil, sweet almond oil, pistachio kernel and wild mango oils. Apply as regular body lotion.

Date Body Scrub For a gentle yet effective exfoliating body scrub, mix date extract with cocoa-butter, sweet almond oil and apricot kernel oil and massage into the skin and rinse off.

Date Compress Mix fresh dates, date kernels, dry myrrh and wax into a fine antiseptic paste. Prepare compress (see box opposite) and bandage the affected area.

THIS PAGE: Dates vary in colour from dark brown to bright yellow and grow in clusters on trees similar to the coconut tree; compresses can be used hot or cold to massage oil onto the body, as they are in Asia, or pressed to the skin to soothe sores and inflamed areas.
OPPOSITE: Date extract can be added to lotions to increase vitamin B content that will nourish the skin.

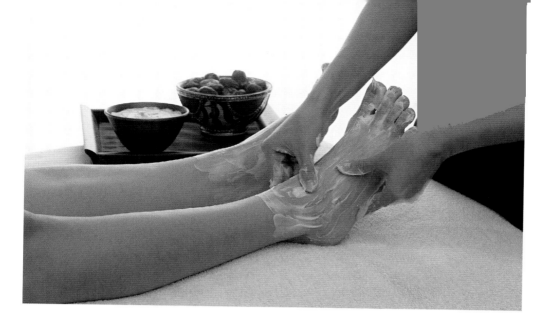

Dates in the Diet

Dates are an excellent source of B vitamins, soluble fibre and iron, copper, magnesium, potassium, zinc and selenium. Research has shown that soluble fibre helps relieve the discomfort of constipation, reduce the body's absorption of cholesterol and keeps blood sugar levels more balanced.

Quick & Easy Serving Ideas

Sweets Dates can be eaten on their own but are also delicious stuffed with an almond, pecan, peanut butter or cottage cheese.

Garnishing Chopped dates can add flavour, texture and sweetness to yoghurt, cereal, rice dishes and all kinds of desserts.

Bread Substitute chopped dates for raisins in bread and muffins for a tasty alternative.

Snacks Use chopped dates as a sandwich spread or to stuff celery.

Flavouring: To uphold Middle Eastern tradition, mix chopped dates into breadcrumbs for stuffings and pilafs. In North African cuisine, dates are used in lamb stews to add a hint of sweetness. For a Moroccan-inspired dish try curried chickpeas, lentils, aubergine and onion topped with chopped dates and roasted peanuts and serve with rice.

Compresses

Compresses have been used for centuries; cold compresses are used for broken non-inflamed skin such as eczema, psoriasis and similar complaints. Heated compresses are used on unbroken skin, to treat conditions such as rheumatism, inflammations, sprains, pain and swelling. Hot compresses should never be directly applied to open wounds.

To make a compress you will need:
A cotton cloth 30 cm x 50 cm (12 inches x 20 inches)
Cling film or surgical tape
Elastic bandage
Woollen cloth
Lay the cloth on a flat surface and spread about 200 ml (7 fl oz/1 cup) of the date, or other compress paste, evenly in the middle of the cotton cloth. Fold each side of the cloth over the content before taping tightly with cling film or surgical tape to ensure the compress is secure. Place the compress on the area to be treated with the cloth side facing towards the skin. Wrap an elastic bandage around and secure the compress to the affected area with tape. The compress may slowly begin to look unsightly as impurities, such as pus, are gradually drawn to the compress from the wound. Compresses should be left in place overnight, but not for more than 10 hours at a time and should never be reused. Once removed the area should be washed with a strong camomile infusion.

Honey

First referred to in ancient Egyptian, Sumerian, Vedic and biblical writings, honey was originally used to pay homage to the gods, embalm the dead and for medicinal cures and beauty rituals. Evidence suggests that it has been collected since 7,000 BC and was considered a food for the rich thereafter.

Designed exclusively for the nourishment of the honey bee, it's estimated that each bee makes just half a teaspoon of honey in its entire lifetime. With tons of honey produced every year, they work hard to supply demand. The bee's work begins with the several miles they must travel to collect nectar from local flowers. Enzymes in the bee saliva then convert the nectar into honey via a simple chemical reaction. They then travel back to the hive to deposit the honey into the honeycomb walls. The rapid movement of the bee wings aerates the honey, decreasing its water content, making it ready to eat.

Bee Pollen Arising from the male germ cell of flowering plants pollen is collected and brought to the hive where the bee adds enzymes and nectar to it. Bee pollen comprises tiny golden yellow to dark brown granules with a delicate flavour and aroma that varies according to the plant pollen it was made from. It is widely used as a nutritive tonic and to desensitize seasonal allergies.

Propolis This is the resin collected by bees from the leaf buds and barks of trees, especially poplar and conifer. Bees use propolis along with beeswax to make their hives. It is a waxy, yellow brown and bitter-flavoured substance that—by virtue of its antibiotic properties that help the hive block bacteria and other micro-organisms—is a widely used anti-microbial agent.

Royal Jelly The worker bees mix honey and bee pollen with enzymes in tiny glands of their throats to produce royal jelly which is used to feed the queen bee. This highly nutritious, thick, milky substance is a renowned nutritional supplement.

THIS PAGE: **Honey has been considered a treat for centuries, it is rich in potassium which helps to balance acid in the body and has traditionally been used as a soother for sore throats and coughs.**
OPPOSITE: **An excellent moisturizer, honey can be applied directly onto the skin to become an effective and revitalizing facial mask.**

Textures and flavours of honey vary depending on which flowers the honey bees choose. Typical choices include heather, alfalfa, clover and the acacia flower. Less common but well-loved flowers conferring their own unique taste on honey are lavender and thyme. The honey bee also produces bee pollen, royal jelly and propolis, all of which share powerful health benefits.

A 15-gram (½-ounce) serving of honey contains about 64 calories (almost all of which is sugar), a trace of protein, iron and certain B vitamins. Actual bee pollen is often considered nature's most perfect food, being a complete protein packed with essential amino acids (the building blocks of protein), B vitamins, minerals and plant hormones. Propolis and royal jelly share similar qualities but have significantly higher levels of biologically active, health-promoting compounds. Being a readily available energy source honey was widely used as a performance enhancer by athletes from the time of the first Olympic Games in Greece in 776 BC.

The health benefits of honey depend very much on its processing and the quality of the flowers used by the bees when collecting pollen. Raw honey (that has not been pasteurized, clarified or filtered) retains more of the beneficial phytochemicals which are lost during the standard processing of the honey.

Honey has long been used as a topical antiseptic for treating ulcers, wounds and burns. A traditional Arabic remedy, that is still popular today, is a spoonful of natural honey taken daily to boost immunity. Also, honey is traditionally mixed with lemon to treat a cough. People from the Near East region (encompassing Jordan and Syria, among others) mix honey with fresh thyme leaves and hot water while those in the Persian gulf (with closer affinity to India) mix it with ginger, a little lime juice and hot water.

Used on the skin, an ancient Arabian cleansing favourite was a face mask made from honey mixed with yoghurt which was applied to the face to deeply exfoliate. The lactic acid in the yoghurt helps to dissolve the outer skin cells and brighten the complexion. Honey water soother was traditionally used to soothe and calm stressed skin and inflamed joints (see page 65).

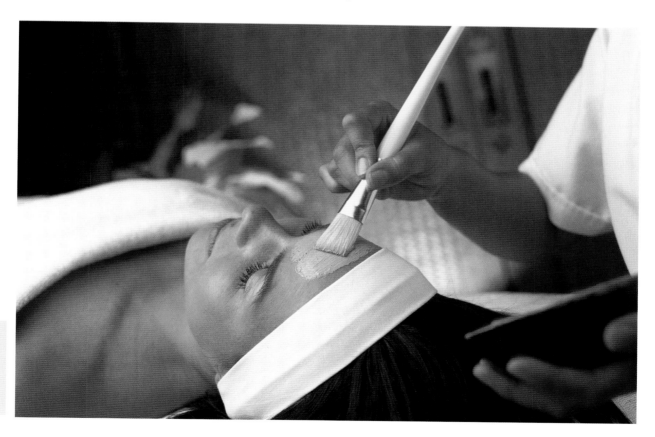

Honey Water Soother

100 g (3½ oz) honey
15 g (½ oz) grated lemon peel
15 g (½ oz) grated orange peel
15 g (½ oz) benzoin (fragrant gum resin)
15 g (½ oz) storax (tree resin)
15 g (½ oz) nutmeg
7 g (⅛ oz) cloves
275 ml (10 fl oz/1 cup) ethyl or alcohol
50 ml (2 fl oz/¼ cup) rosewater
50 ml (2 fl oz/¼ cup) elderflower water

Pour the honey into a glass jar and add the lemon and orange peel, benzoin, storax, nutmeg and cloves. Stir to blend. Add remaining ingredients and beat together. Place the liquid in the jar and shake thoroughly. Allow the mixture to stand for 3 days, shaking frequently. Filter and bottle before using on face and hands.

Other Simple Honey-Based Remedies

Upset Stomach A glass of warm water mixed with 1 tbsp of honey and 1 tbsp of cider vinegar should be sipped slowly to relieve pain.

Indigestion Prepare a syrup using 1 tbsp each of cider vinegar and honey. Swallow a teaspoon before slowly sipping a glass of hot water. This should be taken as needed.

Diarrhoea Mix 1 tbsp of honey with 200 ml (7 fl oz/ 1 cup) of fresh barley water. Drink half of the mixture when necessary.

Stomach Cramps Prepare a syrup by mixing 1 tsp of honey, 1 tsp of cider vinegar and 1 tbsp of calcium lactate. Take 1 tbsp once a day.

Chronic Fatigue Mix 2 tsps of cider vinegar with 350 g (12 oz) honey. Take 2 tsps of the mixture at night before retiring.

Insect Bites Take one part honey to two parts lukewarm water. Add a teaspoon of cinnamon powder and mix thoroughly into a paste. Gently massage on the infected area. Irritation should subside within a few minutes.

Hair Loss Mix together a little hot olive oil, 1 tbsp of honey and 1 tbsp of cinnamon powder to make a paste. Apply to the head before bathing, leaving in place for about 15 minutes so that the hair can absorb the nutrients, before washing off.

Toothache Make a paste of 1 tsp of cinnamon powder and 5 tsps of honey and apply directly onto the aching tooth. This may be applied 3 times a day until the pain recedes.

Cold Mix 1 tbsp of lukewarm honey with 1 tsp of cinnamon powder. Take daily for 3 days to cure a cold and blocked sinuses.

Honey and Orange 'Pick-Me-Up'

225 g (8 oz/1 cup) plain non-fat yoghurt
1 orange peeled, sectioned and seeded
1 tbsp lemon juice
1 tbsp honey
½ tsp of grated orange rind

Process all the ingredients in a blender until smooth and drink as needed

Honey Cough Syrup

1 tbsp liquorice root
1 tbsp crushed anise seeds
1 tbsp dried thyme leaves
350 g (12 oz) honey

Gently simmer the liquorice root and crushed anise seeds in 2 cups of water for 15 minutes in a covered pot. Remove from heat. Add dried thyme leaves, cover and steep until it cools to room temperature. Strain. Add honey and gently warm the tea to completely dissolve the honey. Store in a covered glass jar in the refrigerator where it will keep for at least three months. Take 1 tablespoon as often as needed.

THIS PAGE: It's said that eating some local honey will sensitize you to the local pollens, making the honey a natural remedy for hay fever and all its symptoms.
OPPOSITE: Honey water soother can act as a skin tonic while plain honey water can be used as an eye lotion to help conjunctivitis and other infections.

Saffron

Saffron is the delicate red stigma (female part of the flower) of a small purple crocus (crocus sativus). It is a member of the lily family and has grass-like leaves and large, purple lily-shaped flowers that generally blossom during the autumn months. In a good year each plant can produce several flowers each of which contains three bright red stigmas joined to a pale yellow style. On harvesting, the stigmas are hand cut from the style and then carefully laid on a sieve and cured over heat until dry to deepen the flavour. Once cured, these saffron pieces resemble very fine red-orange threads. It is a painstaking, time-consuming and expensive process as up to 5,000 flowers yield just 25 grams (1 ounce) of the spice—the equivalent of 80,000 flowers (240,000 stigmas) to produce 450 grams (1 pound).

The Ebers Papyrus—considered the most important medical treatise of ancient Egypt—speaks of the medicinal properties of saffron, qualities also noted by both Hippocrates and Galen, who attributed to the spice the ability to improve digestion, eliminate flatulence, act as an antispasmodic and cough suppressant and prevent colic in infants. Furthermore, in ayurvedic medicine, saffron has been used for centuries for alleviating menstrual disorders, impotence, headaches, urinary and digestive problems and overall lack of vitality. Treasured by the ancient Greeks and Romans who called the spice krokos (from crocus, the name of saffron flower) and karkom respectively, saffron appears in the writings of Homer, who lies both Zeus and Jupiter on beds of saffron in order to increase their sexual appetite. Reputed to be so powerful it could corrupt vestal virgins, the spice was widely used to revitalize revellers at the thermal baths. Currently saffron is commercially produced in Morocco, Kashmir, Spain, Italy, Greece and most notably in Iran.

Historically saffron has been used as an aphrodisiac, diaphoretic (to induce sweating), carminative (to prevent gas) and to bring on menstruation. Although there is no solid supporting evidence, some modern research suggests that the spice may protect people against certain forms of cancer, memory loss and heart disease. The spice contains a dark orange, water-soluble carotene called crocin which is responsible for much of its golden colour, antioxidant and possible anti-carcinogenic effects.

Saffron's more modern name Za'faran (the Arabic word for yellow), is given as a gift and today in the Middle East, saffron threads are commonly blended with sandalwood in an oil-based perfume called zafran attar. This ointment is highly valued as a relaxant and headache cure.

The bright red saffron threads are pure alchemy—a mere pinch turns a simple dish into gold. Its brilliant colour, exotic and intense flavour means a pinch goes a long way in many classic Middle Eastern and North African dishes.

Saffron threads are available both whole or ground into a powder. Unless purchased from a reputable source, the whole threads are the best choice as the buyer is able to check that the style (which, when dry, curls up against the stigma) has been cut away, leaving a piece of red stigma up to 1.5 centimetres (½ inch) in length. If buying the powdered version, ensure it is packaged in an airtight tin container to protect the saffron from moisture and light. Saffron powder can be added directly to recipes where its flavour and aroma are immediately released. Saffron threads must first be immersed in an alcoholic, acidic or hot liquid for a minimum of 20 minutes to release their flavour. Either powdered or as threads saffron should be stored in an opaque airtight container in a cool, dry and dark place. High quality saffron will maintain its potency for several years.

Quick & Easy Serving Ideas

- Just a pinch of saffron is enough to transform any fish soup or stew into a rich, golden delicacy (for example, the classic French bouillabaisse).
- A hint of saffron works wonders with rice, as exemplified by the famous Spanish paella, a spicy long-grain rice dish with seafood or chicken.
- Add saffron and cinnamon to whole milk or yoghurt and honey for a simple version of lassi (the famous Indian yoghurt drink).
- Crush a tiny piece of saffron into a glass of champagne or sparkling wine or apple cider for a golden elixir.
- Coffee spiced with saffron and cardamom or milk tea prepared with a pinch of saffron make classic traditional Arabic welcome drinks.

Milk

The earliest found record purporting to the use of animals' milk as a food was unearthed in a temple in the Euphrates Valley near Babylon, where an archaeologist found a wall painting believed to be

THIS PAGE: **Non-fat, dry milk powder can be used to make up a luxurious, Cleopatra-style milk bath at home (see recipe on page 68).**
OPPOSITE: **Saffron crocuses grow across the Middle East, especially in Iran.**

protein, 6.5 grams (1/8 ounce) fat including fat-soluble vitamins A, D, E and K and about 240 mg calcium. In view of the rather high fat content, reduced fat and skimmed milk options are the preferred choice of the health-conscious. Fermented milks and yoghurt contain health promoting bacteria

about 5,000 years old depicting the practice of drinking milk. In ancient Egypt milk consumption was a sign of wealth and status. But it was the history of milk production in the US many years later that was especially significant with the major commercial development of milk taking place in the later part of the 19th century with the widespread adoption of pasteurization for destroying bacteria, moulds and other micro-organisms.

Cow's milk, and its by-products cheese and yoghurt, have long been valued for their nutritional benefits which revolve around the high protein and calcium content. A 200 ml (7 fl oz/1 cup) glass of milk provides 120 calories, 6.6 grams (1/8 ounce)

Home Milk Bath

For a taste of Cleopatra's luxury indulge in a scented milk bath in the home. Rather than using gallons of whole milk, non-fat dry milk is the basis of this bathing treat. The cleansing properties of the milk combine beautifully with the soothing power of baking soda for calming dry and irritated skin. To make the bathing experience more sensual, an assortment of herbs and flowers can be added to scent the bathing mix. Choose from rose petals, lavender, lemon balm, scented geraniums or rosemary to make the bath truly special. Dry herbs are best, as fresh herbs can combine with the dry milk and become mouldy.

750 g (1 lb 10 oz) non-fat dry milk
250 g (9 oz) baking soda
3–4 cups of dried herbs
Blend dry milk powder and baking soda thoroughly in a large bowl. Spread a layer in a large plastic container. Cover with a layer of dried herbs. Continue adding layers of milk and herbs, ending with a layer of herbs. Shake the container to remove excess air pockets. Seal and store mixture for 2–3 weeks to allow the herbal fragrance to seep into the milk powder. Pour the mixture through a sieve to remove the dried herbs. Discard the dried herbs. Store the milk bath mixture in airtight glass jars. If it's for a gift, place an extra layer of dried herbs on top of the jar for decoration. When using, simply pour one cup of the mixture under the tap while filling the bath. Soak for at least 20 minutes and dream of languid evenings sailing the Nile.

THIS PAGE: **A milk bath can easily be prepared at home, the milk will encourage smoother skin and help to ease skin irritations such as eczema and psoriasis.**
OPPOSITE: **Milk and honey have been used on the skin for centuries.**

which are a prerequisite for intestinal health. Milk is one of the richest sources of calcium in the modern diet which is essential for the maturation and ongoing healthy growth and development of skin cells and teeth. Magnesium, another mineral in milk, works together with calcium on the smooth conduction of nerves throughout the body.

In beauty, Cleopatra is said to have bathed in a bath of milk and whey (rich in linoleic acid), olive oil and honey; the combination will help dry stressed or sensitive skin. Today, the legend lives on with beauty experts advocating the benefits of milk baths, due to the high content of calcium, potassium, sodium and magnesium for improving skin tone and texture. Also, the exfoliating benefits of the yoghurt and honey face masks of ancient Arabia are availed of in many skin-cleansing products and are widely used in spas around the world.

Quick & Easy Serving Ideas

- Using a food processor, blend favourite fruits (either fresh or frozen) with milk or yoghurt. You can add honey to taste and serve as deliciously nourishing breakfast or snack any time of the day.
- Add 1 cup of milk and some raisins, cinnamon and nutmeg to a pot of cooked rice to make a delicious rice pudding.
- For easy sleep and sweet dreams, ayurvedic medicine recommends drinking warmed milk with a pinch of nutmeg one hour before bed.
- For the perfect winter warmer, combine milk with drinking chocolate or cocoa powder and warm over a low heat. For a healthier version, use dark chocolate, which contains up to four times the antioxidants found in tea.

Figs

The world's first cultivated tree, the fig tree comes from the moraceae family and can be traced back to the Bible and other ancient writings. A native of the Middle East and Mediterranean, the fig tree is believed to have been farmed in Egypt before being carried to Greece where they were held in such high regard that laws were enacted preventing any export of the finest quality figs.

Figs grow on the ficus tree (ficus carica), which is related to the mulberry family. They have a very sweet taste with a chewy texture to their flesh and skin and a crunchiness to their seeds. Fresh figs are delicate and perish easily so most figs are dried, either by exposure to sunlight or through an artificial process that creates a sweet and nutritious dried fruit that can be enjoyed throughout the year.

Figs are naturally high in simple sugars, minerals and fibre. A 100 gram (3½ ounce) serving of dried figs (or about 8–10) provides approximately 250 calories and 10 grams (¼ ounce) of fibre. With such rich fibre content, figs nourish and tone the intestines, while fig leaves have been found to help stabilize blood sugar levels in the body.

When choosing fresh figs, select those that are plump and tender, with a rich deep colour and free from bruises. They should be kept covered in the refrigerator on a paper-towel lined plate where they will stay fresh for about 2 days and should not be washed until ready to eat. Dried figs can stay fresh for several months if they are kept wrapped in a cool dry place or in the refrigerator.

Quick & Easy Serving Ideas

- Dried figs can be used in jams and fruit dishes.
- Purée ripe figs for a tasty sandwich filler or use to complement chicken, tofu and vegetable dishes.
- Fresh or fried figs can be added to breakfast cereals for added sweetness and goodness.
- Poached figs in juice or red wine are delicious served with yoghurt or frozen desserts.
- Fresh figs are a perfect accompaniment to all kinds of cheeses.
- Another cheese snack is fresh figs stuffed with goat's cheese and chopped almonds.

Tea

Brewing and drinking tea is considered an art form with tea ceremonies celebrated with reverence all around the world, from China, India and Japan to Africa and the Middle East. It's believed that tea was originally discovered over 5,000 years ago. Legend has it that tea leaves blew into a Chinese emperor's pot of boiling water. Later, the drink spread through to the Far and Middle East and from there to Europe and the United States.

THIS PAGE: Figs can be eaten to protect the body against cancer and heart disease, and the high sugar content will help to increase energy levels.
OPPOSITE: Bedouin taking time to relax in the desert and take in the serene surroundings with a cup of mint tea.

Both green and black tea come from the same plant (camellia sinensis), a 1-metre (3-foot) shrub. The main difference between them is down to the manufacturing process. In the production of black tea, the leaves are allowed to oxidize as enzymes present in the tea convert the polyphenols into substances with much less biological activity. In contrast, green tea is produced by lightly steaming the fresh cut leaf. Steaming prevents the oxidation and the polyphenols remain intact thereby conferring health benefits. Oolong tea is partially oxidized. White tea is actually green tea but the new, unopened buds are picked and steamed or dried. The resulting tea is pale yellow in colour, low in caffeine with a mild and slightly sweeter taste than green tea.

Research has found that, due to its higher content of polyphenols, green tea is a powerful immune booster and can help protect the body against certain forms of cancer, especially those of the gastrointestinal tract (stomach, small intestine, pancreas and colon), prostate, lung and breast cancer. Regular consumption of green tea has also been found to help maintain healthy, glowing skin.

Additionally, both green and black varieties contain significant levels of vitamins C, D, K and B2 (riboflavin) as well as some calcium, magnesium, iron, zinc and sodium and fluoride. Further, 200 ml (7 fl oz/1 cup) of tea contains just 1 calorie and is free from protein and fat.

Caffeine Content

Drink per 200ml (6oz)	Milligrams of caffeine
Drip coffee	60-180
Espresso	60-90
Black tea	25-110
Oolong tea	12-55
Green tea	8-16

Mint Tea

Mint tea is the ideal refresher for the hot and dry Middle Eastern climate and is part of the Arabs' daily ritual. Traditionally, green tea and mint leaves are brewed together and then poured into a glass. Fresh mint leaves are sometimes added along with generous helpings of sugar. The Arabian tooth is certainly a sweet one.

When serving the tea, it is poured from a distance (lifting one hand up high and pouring) so foam appears on the top of the tea.

Cardamom Coffee

For a true Arabian twist to coffee simply add cardamom pods to the coffee pot—it makes a very distinctive and delicious cup of coffee.

Cardamom is one of the oldest known spices. The seeds were chewed by the ancient Egyptians— an ancient tooth cleaner; the Greeks and Romans used it as a perfume; and it featured regularly in the *Arabian Nights* for its aphrodisiac qualities while the ancient Indians used it as a cure for obesity.

True cardamom (elettaria cardamomum) is a perennial plant with simple erect stems (or canes) that can reach a height of up to 3.5 metres (12 feet). The small green fruit contains up to 18 seeds, which can be used whole or ground as a spice.

Medicinally, cardamom is primarily used as a digestive aid for indigestion and flatulence. While its main gastronomic role is in curry powder, it is also found in desserts and coffee. For beauty purposes it can be used as a fragrance in soaps, lotions and perfumes. Cardamom essential oil blends well with frankincense and other aphrodisiac oils such as patchouli, rose and cedarwood.

Senna

Senna (cassia angustifolia) is a small shrub, with pale, yellowish-green, olive leaves, that grows in the upper Nile regions of Africa and the Arabian peninsula. Ancient Egyptian doctors used Senna over 3,500 years ago to treat their royal patients and other members of the elite society. During the Crusades, Senna was introduced to Europe and it has been widely used ever since, either on its own or in conjunction with other aromatic herbs.

Today the herb is used as a laxative with its active ingredients the basis of a number of commercial products. Both its leaves and seeds help relieve constipation by stimulating the colon and speeding along the passage of its contents. Senna is available as a crushed herb, a liquid or a powdered extract.

Senna Tea: This bitter tasting herbal laxative should produce bowel movement within 6–12 hours. Pour hot (but not boiling) water over ½–¼ tsp of crushed senna herb. Steep for about 10 minutes, strain and drink, preferably before bedtime. The tea can be sweetened with honey if desired.

Senna tea can also be prepared by steeping crushed senna for 12 hours in cold water and then straining. It is believed that preparing senna as a cold tea produces less resin in the tea thereby decreasing the risk of abdominal cramps.

THIS PAGE: **Mint tea is everywhere in the Middle East and is a favourite of the bedouin who drink it to refresh after their arduous journey.**
OPPOSITE: **Coffee is taken seriously, with strict traditions for pouring and drinking, traditionally made with cardamom it can also be sweetened.**

Spa Cuisine

Arabia is a bounty of natural goodness. With a huge variety of healthy, locally grown fruit and vegetables, such as freshly picked lemons and plump peppers and pumpkins, Middle Eastern cuisine delights the palate with its own distinctive taste. To add some substance to its remarkable flavours, Arabic cuisine uses pulses and pastes to complete the dish, for example the quintessentially Arabian tabouleh and hummus. For a meaty alternative, lamb is favoured as kebabs or in the famous kibbeh, and chicken is loved across the region cooked in various ways.

No one disputes the healthiness of Arabian cuisine that has evolved over time into the opulent, fusion and modern versions we see in the following pages.

The Opulent Kitchen

MODERN ARABIAN INDULGENCE

For centuries, Arabia has taken pride in its innate grandness and, from Cleopatra's decadence to today's five-star hotels of Dubai, food has always been a key indulgence. Now, the lavish style of spas, hotels and resorts across Arabia has given birth to a new wave of modern Arabian cuisine. Some of the world's most precious food resources are used to sate the most discerning of tastes, from Iranian beluga and osetra caviar to quail eggs, from fleur de sel to gold embellishments. The following recipes, by Chef Jean Paul Naquin of the Burj Al Arab, ensure these healthy meals are easily executed. They will introduce seven-star dining into the home yet remain reassuring for the health-conscious.

Caviar is a pivotal ingredient in the Burj Al Arab's opulent seafood cuisine. Fresh from nature, caviar is packed full of energy and protein. Vitamins A, C, B2, B6 and B12 and the high content of folic acid mean caviar is beneficial in any diet, even the most extravagant ones.

Steamed Line-Caught Sea Bass with Asparagus, Egg Sabayon & Iranian Caviar

Serves 4
Kilocalories 313 kcal > Protein 35 g > Carbohydrate 5 g > Total Fat 17 g

400 g (14 oz) green asparagus
400 g (14 oz) white asparagus
600 g (1 lb 5 oz) wild sea bass fillet
salt and ground white pepper to taste
4 tsp lemon juice
10 g (¼ oz) lemon zest, grated
4 egg yolks
60 g (2¼ oz) Iranian golden osetra caviar
4 tsp olive oil
15 g (½ oz) chives, chopped

Peel and cook green asparagus in boiling salted water for approximately 5 minutes or until slightly tender. Remove and refresh in iced water. Reserve 12 tbsp of the cooking liquid for preparation of the sabayon. Drain asparagus, cut into 6 cm (2½ inch) lengths and set aside. Peel white asparagus and shave, length-wise, into thin slices. Divide sea bass fillets into 4 equal portions, season and steam for 6 minutes. To prepare sabayon, pour reserved asparagus cooking liquid into a mixing bowl with lemon juice, half the lemon zest, egg yolks and some seasoning. Place the mixing bowl in a bain-marie and whip until mixture is foamy. Adjust seasoning to taste and keep warm until ready to serve. Toss white asparagus shavings with caviar and olive oil and season. Divide equally among 4 serving plates. Heat green asparagus in a steamer and arrange with a gold-plated frame on each plate. Place sea bass on the plates, pour over sabayon, sprinkle over chives and remaining lemon zest and serve.

Hammour Carpaccio with Caviar, Lemon Yoghurt Dressing & Crispy Arabic Bread

Serves 4
Kilocalories 308 kcal > Protein 28 g > Carbohydrate 21 g > Total Fat 13 g

325 g (11½ oz) hammour (or grouper) fillet
fleur de sel and ground black pepper to taste
4 tsp olive oil
120 g (4¼ oz) low-fat yoghurt
4 tsp lemon juice
10 g (¼ oz) lemon zest
60 g (2¼ oz) Iranian beluga caviar
160 g (5⅝ oz) Arabic flat bread, toasted and cut into squares
85 g (3 oz) micro-greens (miniature rocket, lettuce)
4 quail eggs, boiled for 3 minutes, refreshed and peeled
10 g (¼ oz) chives, chopped

Slice fish fillet thinly. Brush the centre of each serving plate lightly with olive oil, arrange fish slices on top and season. Drizzle over remaining oil. Mix low-fat yoghurt with lemon juice and zest and spoon over the fish carpaccio. Place a steel ring on each plate and fill the rings with caviar. Carefully remove rings to leave caviar in a neat pile. Add toasted Arabic bread, micro-greens, quail eggs, chives, remaining fleur de sel and pepper, and serve.

Omani Lobster Tournedos, Vegetable Tian, Lemongrass Bisque & Garlic Smoothie

Serves 4
Kilocalories 475 kcal > Protein 40 g > Carbohydrate 15 g > Total Fat 29 g

Vegetable tian:
2 tbsp olive oil
15 g (½ oz) garlic, chopped
120 g (4¼ oz) red pepper, peeled and diced
120 g (4¼ oz) yellow pepper, peeled and diced
120 g (4¼ oz) yellow courgette, diced
120 g (4¼ oz) marrow, diced
85 g (3 oz) onion, peeled and diced
salt and pepper to taste
120 g (4¼ oz) tomato, peeled and diced

Lemongrass bisque:
40 g (1½ oz) lemongrass, finely chopped
400 ml (14 fl oz/1⅔ cups) lobster bisque
salt and pepper to taste

Garlic smoothie:
60 g (2¼ oz) garlic, peeled
40 g (1½ oz) egg white
2 tsp lemon juice
40 g (1½ oz) ice cubes
5 g (⅛ oz) salt
4 tsp corn oil

Omani lobster tournedos:
500 g (1 lb 2 oz) Omani lobster tail, net weight
(750 g (1 lb 10 oz) with shell)
4 tbsp olive oil

Garnishing:
40 g (1½ oz) baby spinach leaves
5 g (⅛ oz) sumac powder
2 tsp olive oil

To prepare the vegetable tian, heat olive oil in a non-stick pan. Add garlic, followed by all the other vegetables except the tomato. Season and sauté for 3 minutes. Add tomato and sauté for another 1 minute. Adjust seasoning to taste and keep warm. To prepare lemongrass bisque, place lemongrass in hot lobster bisque and allow to infuse for 5 minutes. Pour bisque through a fine sieve, adjust seasoning to taste and keep warm. To prepare the garlic smoothie, blend garlic in a food processor and add egg white, lemon juice, ice and salt. Blend until smooth. With the processor still running, add corn oil through the funnel and continue blending until thoroughly mixed. Set aside. Using a bread knife, cut each lobster tail, with shell still attached, into 4 medallions. Heat olive oil in a frying pan over medium heat. Add lobster medallions and cook for 3 minutes each side. Do this in batches if necessary. Remove from heat and keep warm. Place 2 steel rings onto each serving plate and spoon vegetable tian into them. Remove the rings carefully. Add lobster medallions and 2 dessert spoons of garlic smoothie per serving. Blend lemongrass bisque with a hand blender to obtain a foam and spoon onto the plates. Add spinach leaves and drizzle with olive oil. Sprinkle sumac powder over garlic emulsion and serve immediately.

Halawat al Jeben, Rosewater Sherbert & Mango

Serves 6
Kilocalories 299 kcal > Protein 4 g > Carbohydrate 61 g > Total Fat 3 g

Crystallized rose petals:
18 red rose petals
1 pasteurized egg white
20 g (¾ oz) castor sugar

Rosewater sherbert:
150 ml (5 fl oz/⅔ cup) rosewater
100 ml (3½ fl oz/⅜ cup) sugar syrup (made with 50 g (1¾ oz)
sugar and 50 ml (2 fl oz/¼ cup) water)
4 tsp lemon juice
pinch of ice cream stabilizer
1 red rose petal

Halawat al jeben:
100 ml (3½ fl oz/⅜ cup) water
75 g (2⅝ oz) sugar
20 g (¾ oz) glucose
75 g (2⅝ oz) semolina
150 g (5½ oz) akawi cheese (salty cheese)
2 tsp rosewater
2 tsp orange blossom water
30 g (1 oz) Lebanese ashta (clotted) cream

Rosewater syrup:
30 g (1 oz) water
30 g (1 oz) sugar syrup
2 tsp rosewater

Garnishing:
700 g (1 lb 9 oz) mango, whole
30 g (1 oz) pistachio nuts, chopped

To prepare the crystallized rose petals, brush each petal with egg white and sprinkle lightly with castor sugar. Place on greaseproof paper and allow to dry for 1 day. To prepare rosewater sherbet, blend all ingredients in a food processor and freeze. To prepare the halawat al jeben (semolina cheese dough), place water, sugar and glucose in a saucepan and bring to a boil. Lower the heat and slowly add semolina, stirring well. Cook for about 2 minutes. Remove from heat and allow to cool. Incorporate akawi cheese, rosewater and orange blossom water to obtain a dough consistency. Roll the dough flat on a lightly oiled surface to prevent it sticking. Spread over a layer of ashta cream and roll to obtain a cylinder 2.5 cm (1 inch) in diameter. Cut into small cylinders 5 cm (2 inches) long. To prepare rosewater syrup, bring water and syrup to a boil. Remove from heat and add rosewater. To serve, peel mango and cut half into small cubes and the other half into thick discs 4 cm (1¾ inch) in diameter. Place 3 discs of mango on a plate, add 2 cylinders of halawat al jeben and a spoon of diced mango. Spoon rosewater sherbert onto each plate and drizzle rosewater syrup on top of the halawat al jeben. Decorate with crystallized rose petals and chopped pistachio nuts. Serve immediately.

The Modern Arabian Kitchen

OLD FAVOURITES WITH A NEW TWIST

Following the culinary traditions of the Levant, there is a deep sense of the Mediterranean with the cuisine's fresh salads and mezze style. Yet, the signature tastes of the Near East feast transport you straight back to the stunning region that encompasses Lebanon, Syria, Jordan and Egypt.

Once the trading link between East and West, this region of the Middle East has witnessed a multitude of different cultures each bringing their own taste and style. Now, centuries later, each country has its own name for each dish but the melting pot of the Near East has converged into one culinary guise.

Chef Jean Paul Naquin of the Burj Al Arab has taken the old Arabian favourites, such as tabouleh, hummus and lebneh and served them with interesting salads and roasted meat, rather than the usual khobiz (Arabic bread). The dishes steer away from the mezze style to healthier versions with all the distinctive flavours of Arabia.

Salad of Diver Scallops with Grilled Aubergine Baba Ganoush & Coriander Dressing

Serves 4
Kilocalories 342 kcal > Protein 20 g > Carbohydrate 9 g > Total Fat 26 g

Baba ganoush:
525 g (1 lb 3 oz) aubergine, left whole
85 g (3 oz) tomato, peeled and diced
40 g (1½ oz) green capsicum, chopped
40 g (1½ oz) yellow capsicum, chopped
40 g (1½ oz) parsley, chopped
40 g (1½ oz) onion, chopped
15 g (½ oz) garlic, chopped
4 tsp olive oil
2 tsp lemon juice
salt to taste

Coriander dressing:
120 g (4¼ oz) coriander leaves
40 g (1½ oz) low-fat yoghurt
4 tsp olive oil

Salad:
120 g (4¼ oz) aubergine, thinly sliced
60 g (2¼ oz) black olives, pitted and finely chopped
40 g (1½ oz) native greens
35 g (1¼ oz) pomegranate seeds
4 tsp olive oil
salt to taste

Sea scallops:
325 g (11½ oz) sea scallops, net weight
salt and pepper to taste
4 tsp olive oil

To prepare baba ganoush, grill aubergines over a medium heat, turning frequently, for about 20 minutes. or until they begin to soften. Increase the heat and continue grilling and turning for about 10 minutes until skins are charred. Allow to cool and remove skins. Place aubergines in a strainer to drain any excess water and cool in the refrigerator. Once cooled, chop aubergines and mix with remaining baba ganoush ingredients. Adjust seasoning to taste and set aside. To prepare dressing, blend all coriander dressing ingredients in a food processor until smooth and transfer to the refrigerator. For the salad, pre-heat oven to 90°C (190°F), brush aubergine slices with olive oil and place on a baking sheet lined with greaseproof paper. Place another sheet of greaseproof paper on top of the aubergine slices and cover with another baking tray. Bake for 2 hours or until aubergine slices are crispy. Remove and season. To prepare sea scallops, season and drizzle with olive oil. Place on a hot grill and cook quickly on both sides until medium done. To serve, place 3 steel rings on each plate, spoon baba ganoush into the rings and remove to leave a neat pile. Place warm sea scallops on each plate. Add aubergine chips, chopped black olives, native greens and pomegranate seeds. Spoon over coriander dressing and serve.

Chicken Breast with Hummus & Native Herbs

Serves 4
Kilocalories 390 kcal > Protein 30 g > Carbohydrate 13 g > Total Fat 24 g

Hummus:
200 g (7 oz) chickpeas
2.5 L (4½ pints) water
1 tsp bicarbonate of soda
160 ml (5 fl oz/²⁄₃ cup) cold water
40 g (1½ oz) tahina (sesame seed paste)
15 g (½ oz) garlic, peeled
10 g (¼ oz) salt
2 tsp lemon juice

Chicken:
250 g (9 oz) chicken breast, skinless
salt and pepper to taste
8 tsp olive oil
125 g (4½ oz) rocket leaves
85 g (3 oz) wild thyme leaves
8 black olives, pitted and chopped
160 g/5⅝ oz red pepper, roasted, peeled and diced

To prepare hummus, soak chickpeas overnight in 1 L (1¾ pints/4 cups) water with bicarbonate of soda. The next day, strain chickpeas and place in a large pan with about 1.5 L (2¾ pints) water. Bring to a boil, lower heat and simmer for 35–45 minutes until chickpeas are tender and the skins come away easily. Strain and wash in cold water to remove skins. Strain again and transfer to the refrigerator. Reserve 24 chickpeas for garnishing. Blend remaining chickpeas in a food processor with cold water, tahina, garlic, salt and lemon juice until smooth. Adjust seasoning to taste and place in the refrigerator. Pre-heat oven to 180°C (360°F). Season chicken and bake with half of the olive oil for approximately 15–20 minutes or until cooked. Remove from heat and allow to rest. Slice length-wise. To serve, arrange hummus and chicken on 4 plates. Scatter over rocket, wild thyme, olives, red pepper and reserved chickpeas. Drizzle remaining olive oil equally over the plates and serve.

Tabouleh with Lemon & Gulf Prawns

Serves 4
Kilocalories 243 kcal > Protein 17 g > Carbohydrate 14 g > Total Fat 14 g

600 g (1 lb 5 oz) live Gulf prawns

Dressing:
4 tsp olive oil
2 tsp lemon juice
salt to taste

Beetroot dressing:
8 tbsp beetroot juice
4 tsp olive oil

Tabouleh:
120 g (4¼ oz) parsley, chopped
85 g (3 oz) bulgur wheat
85 g (3 oz) tomato, diced
40 g (1½ oz) onion, chopped
20 g (¾ oz) mint leaves, chopped
10 g (¼ oz) lemon zest
2 tsp lemon juice
salt and pepper to taste

Garnishing:
160 g (5⅝ oz) orange, cut into segments
85 g (3 oz) lemon, cut into segments
60 g (2¼ oz) parsley leaves
10 g (¼ oz) lemon zest, julienned

Steam prawns for approximately 5 minutes until cooked and chill in iced water. Drain excess water, shell and de-vein prawns. Reserve in the refrigerator. Mix together all dressing ingredients, adjust seasoning to taste and reserve. To make beetroot dressing, reduce the beetroot juice by half over a medium heat and incorporate olive oil. Just before serving, mix all tabouleh ingredients thoroughly and adjust seasoning to taste. Brush the edges of 4 serving plates with beetroot dressing. Place a rectangular frame 10 cm by 3 cm (4 inches by 1¼ inches) in the centre of each plate and fill with tabouleh. Remove the frames carefully. Add prawns, parsley leaves, orange and lemon segments and lemon zest to the plates. Spoon over dressing and serve.

Lebneh Sandwiches with Mint & Olive Salad

Serves 4
Kilocalories 321 kcal > Protein 10 g > Carbohydrate 17 g > Total Fat 25 g

Lebneh sandwiches:
250 g (9 oz) lebneh (Lebanese yoghurt-based cheese)
40 g (1½ oz) bulgur wheat
40 g (1½ oz) fresh mint leaves, finely chopped
10 g (¼ oz) garlic, finely chopped
250 g (9 oz) cucumber
200 g (7 oz) carrot

Olive salad:
85 g (3 oz) green olives, pitted and sliced
40 g (1½ oz) chilli paste
40 g (1½ oz) pine nuts, roasted
4 tsp olive oil

Garnishing:
15 g (½ oz) black olives, chopped
5 g (⅛ oz) sumac powder
60 g (2¼ oz) zata leaves
20 g (¾ oz) fresh mint leaves
2 tsp olive oil
20 g (¾ oz) pine nuts, roasted

To prepare lebneh sandwiches, place lebneh in a mixing bowl, add bulgur wheat, mint leaves and garlic and mix well. Slice cucumber into 9 cm by 3 cm (3½ inches by 1¼ inches) rectangles of 2 mm (⅛ inch) thickness. Using a piping bag with a round nozzle, pipe lebneh filling onto 1 slice of cucumber. Top with another slice of cucumber to form a sandwich. Repeat the process to obtain 8 sandwiches. Arrange them vertically in pairs onto 4 serving plates. Peel carrot and cut into 7 cm by 2 cm (2¾ inch by 1 inch) rectangles of 2 mm (⅛ inch) thickness. Place carrot slices into a small steel ring. Fill the centre with lebneh filling and remove the ring. Repeat to obtain 8 cylinders. Add 2 cylinders to each plate. For each plate, sprinkle 1 cylinder with chopped black olives. Cut 4 more rectangles of carrot and place 1 on the edge of each plate. Pipe a cylinder of lebneh filling onto each rectangle and dust with sumac powder. Mix all ingredients for olive salad together and spoon onto the plates. To garnish, gently toss leaves in olive oil and add pine nuts, arrange on plates and serve.

Roasted Chicken Wings, Carrot Bouchons & Cumin Cappuccino

Serves 4
Kilocalories 414 kcal > Protein 33 g > Carbohydrate 16 g > Total Fat 25 g

Roasted chicken wings:
750 g (1 lb 10 oz) free-range chicken wings, bone-in
800 ml (1⅓ pints/3⅜ cups) red wine vinegar
20 g (¾ oz) honey
10 g (¼ oz) red chilli, chopped
1 tbsp olive oil
10 g (¼ oz) salt
5 g (⅛ oz) ground pepper

Carrot bouchons & smoothie:
450 g (1 lb) carrots
200 g (7 oz) low-fat yoghurt
4 tsp olive oil
salt and ground white pepper to taste

Cumin cappuccino:
400 ml (14 fl oz/1⅔ cups) milk
10 g (¼ oz) chicken stock powder
10 g (¼ oz) cumin seeds

Garnishing:
4 tbsp brown chicken jus (from
the roasted chicken wings)
60 g (2¼ oz) beetroot leaves
10 g (¼ oz) cumin seeds

To prepare roasted chicken, marinate chicken wings in red
wine vinegar, honey, chilli, oil, salt and pepper and place in the
refrigerator for 1 hour. For the carrot bouchons, peel carrots and
cook in boiling salted water until tender. Remove and cool in iced
water. Drain and chop into 4 cm- (1¾ inch-) long pieces. Using an
apple corer, cut out 24 cylinders from the carrot and set aside. To
prepare the carrot smoothie, blend carrot trimmings in a food
processor with yoghurt and olive oil until smooth and adjust
seasoning to taste. To prepare chicken wings, wrap each in
aluminium foil. Heat 1–2 tbsps olive oil in a frying pan over a high
heat. Place chicken parcels in pan and cook for about 7 minutes
or until golden brown, turning frequently to prevent them from
burning. Remove from heat and add carrot cylinders to the pan to
keep warm. Drain 4 tbsp chicken jus from the parcels, heat and set
aside. Place all cumin cappuccino ingredients into a saucepan and
bring to a boil. Remove from the heat and blend with a hand mixer
to obtain a light foam. To serve, spoon carrot smoothie onto the
serving plates. Add chicken wings and carrot cylinders. Spoon over
chicken jus and cumin cappuccino. Decorate with beetroot leaves
and cumin seeds and serve immediately.

Pomegranate Granité, Ashta Phyllo Crunch & Orange Salad

Serves 6
Kilocalories 661 kcal > Protein 6 g > Carbohydrate 47 g > Total Fat 51 g

Ashta phyllo crunch:
200 g (7 oz) phyllo dough
10 g (¼ oz) butter, melted
15 g (½ oz) castor sugar
500 g (1 lb 2 oz) ashta (clotted) cream
20 g (¾ oz) icing sugar
15 g (½ oz) orange zest, grated

Pomegranate granité:
600 ml (1 pint/2½ cups) fresh pomegranate juice
30 g (1 oz) icing sugar
4 tsp lemon juice

Garnishing:
70 g (2½ oz) raspberry coulis
4 navel oranges, cut into segments
2 tbsp pomegranate seeds
10 g (¼ oz) fresh mint
2 vanilla beans, each cut length-wise into 3

To prepare crispy phyllo, pre-heat oven to 170°C (340°F). Brush a sheet of phyllo with butter and sprinkle castor sugar on top. Cover with another sheet of phyllo and roll over with a rolling pin to combine the two sheets. Cut into identical rectangles 4 cm by 9 cm (1¾ inch by 3½ inches) and place on a baking tray lined with greaseproof paper. Bake for about 10 minutes or until light brown and crisp. Set aside. To prepare filling, mix ashta cream, icing sugar and orange zest until well combined. Pour mixture onto a tray and spread evenly to 1 cm (½ inch) thickness. Allow to cool and cut into 2 cm by 9 cm (1 inch by 3½ inch) rectangles. (If mixture is too soft to cut, place in the freezer for 1 hour first.) Reserve in the refrigerator until serving. To prepare granité, combine pomegranate juice, icing sugar and lemon juice. Pour mixture onto a flat tray and freeze for 5 hours. Using a spoon, scrape fine ice crystals from the frozen mixture and reserve in the freezer until serving. To assemble ashta pastries, place a phyllo rectangle on a serving plate and place a rectangle of ashta filling on top. Cover with a phyllo rectangle and place another ashta rectangle on top. Cover with another phyllo rectangle and press down lightly so that the layers hold together. Repeat the process to obtain 6 servings. Using a plastic squeezy bottle, pour raspberry coulis onto the serving plates. Place ashta pastry in the centre of each plate, add orange segments to one side and a glass filled with granité on the other. Garnish with pomegranate seeds, fresh mint, vanilla bean and serve immediately.

Arabia's Fusion Kitchen

A COSMOPOLITAN APPROACH

A genuine fusion style will adopt the culinary favourites and embellish them with complementary tastes from another cuisine. Here, the chefs from Six Senses Spa at Madinat Jumeirah have shared its healthy cuisine that bears all the hallmarks of Arabian culinary tradition but with a distinct twist. Take for example the vine leaf parcels. This dish is a very traditional and common way of eating meat across the Middle East. Here the leaf has been used to wrap an Italian-style lobster risotto with tomato salsa. As well, the lentil soup encompasses the flavours of the Egyptian herb of cumin but the dish moves in another seafood direction with the addition of scallop and caviar.

The Six Senses cuisine aims to provide food that will take you on a sensory journey; their philosophy is a holistic one that takes into account wellness of both the body and mind. Strongly recommended by the chefs are fresh juices and natural produce that boost energy levels and improve general health.

Salad of Steamed Chicken with Bean Sprouts, Carrot, Spring Onion & Soy Sesame Dressing

Serves 4
Kilocalories 671 kcal > Protein 43 g > Carbohydrate 32 g > Total Fat 42 g

Dressing:
60 g (2¼ oz) soft brown sugar
4 tbsp lemon juice
125 ml (4 fl oz/½ cup) soy sauce
150 ml (5 fl oz/⅔ cup) corn oil
150 ml (5 fl oz/⅔ cup) sesame oil

Salad:
500 g (1 lb 2 oz) boneless chicken breast, skinned
200 g (7 oz) bean sprouts
200 g (7 oz) carrot, peeled and julienned
120 g (4¼ oz) enoki mushrooms
120 g (4¼ oz) shallots, peeled and sliced
85 g (3 oz) spring onions, finely chopped
60 g (2¼ oz) red chillies, julienned
salt and pepper to taste

To prepare the dressing, dissolve sugar in lemon juice and soy sauce and slowly blend in oils until well mixed. To prepare chicken, steam for 10 minutes, or until cooked. Allow to cool and shred into fine strips. Toss with remaining salad ingredients and add dressing. Check and adjust seasoning to taste, and serve.

Lentil Soup with Seared Scallop, Quail Egg, Caviar & Herb Toast

Serves 4
Kilocalories 572 kcal > Protein 24 g > Carbohydrate 37 g > Total Fat 38 g

400 g (14 oz) red lentils
2 tbsp olive oil
250 g (9 oz) carrot, peeled and diced
250 g (9 oz) celery, peeled and diced
250 g (9 oz) onion, peeled and diced
1 tsp cumin powder
1 L (1¾ pt/4 cups) vegetable stock
4 scallops, about 40 g (1½ oz) each
4 quail eggs
4 x 2 cm- (1 inch-) thick slices of focaccia bread
120 g (4¼ oz) butter, melted
2 tsp chilli powder
40 g (1½ oz) fresh parsley, chopped
4 tsp coriander powder
20 g (¾ oz) spring onion, julienned
4 tsp Iranian beluga caviar
salt and pepper to taste

To prepare lentil soup, sift through lentils and remove any grit or
small stones. Rinse and drain. Heat oil in a large soup pan over a
medium heat, sauté diced carrot, celery and onion for 3–5 minutes,
until softened but not brown. Add drained lentils and sauté for
3 minutes. Add cumin powder and vegetable stock and bring to a
boil. Lower heat and simmer until lentils are soft. Blend soup in a
food processor until smooth and pass through a sieve back into the
pan. Adjust seasoning and keep warm. To prepare scallops, heat a
non-stick pan and sear scallops rapidly on both sides until golden
brown in colour. Remove from heat and set aside. To prepare quail
eggs, wrap each in cling water and poach in simmering water for
3 minutes until just set. Next, brush focaccia with melted butter,
sprinkle with chilli powder and parsley and crisp under a hot grill.
Pour hot soup into 4 soup bowls, place scallop in the centre of each
and sprinkle with coriander and spring onion. Top with quail egg
and 1 tsp caviar, season to taste and serve with herb toast.

Vine Leaf Parcels filled with Lobster Risotto & Tomato Salsa

Serves 4
Kilocalories 476 kcal > Protein 41 g > Carbohydrate 41 g > Total Fat 16 g

Vine leaf parcels:
1 lobster tail (weight 650 g (1 lb 7 oz))
500 g (1 lb 2 oz) risotto (arborio or carnaroli) rice, uncooked
20 g (¾ oz) butter
120 g (4¼ oz) onion, peeled and diced
60 g (2¼ oz) garlic, peeled and chopped
120 g (4¼ oz) marscapone cheese
1 tsp ground nutmeg
4 tsp lemon juice
salt and pepper to taste
12 vine leaves

Tomato salsa:
250 g (9 oz) plum tomatoes
40 g (1½ oz) shallots, peeled and chopped
10 g (¼ oz) mint leaves, shredded
250 ml (9 fl oz/1 cup) olive oil
4 tsp lemon juice
salt and pepper to taste

Basil oil:
150 g (5½ oz) fresh basil leaves
250 ml (9 fl oz/1 cup) olive oil

Balsamic reduction:
250 ml (9 fl oz/1 cup) balsamic vinegar

Salad:
100 g (3½ oz) yellow frisée lettuce
40 g (1½ oz) daikon cress
40 g (1½ oz) shiso cress
10 g (¼ oz) pink peppercorns, crushed

To prepare risotto, cook lobster tail in boiling water for 4–5 minutes or until just done. Cut tail in half. Reserve half and dice other half. Set aside. Steam risotto rice for 15 minutes, until al dente. Set aside. Next, heat a pan and add butter, onion, and garlic and sauté over medium-low heat, until softened. Once soft, add diced lobster and risotto and mix well. Next, add marscapone cheese and nutmeg to the risotto and cook over low heat until rice has absorbed most of the liquid. Add lemon juice and season to taste. Allow risotto to cool then wrap in vine leaves. To prepare tomato salsa, blanch tomatoes in boiling water for 1 minute, drain and plunge into cold water. Skin and dice tomatoes and mix with remaining salsa ingredients. Season to taste. To prepare basil oil, blanch basil leaves in boiling water, drain quickly and refresh immediately in cold water. Gently squeeze dry and blend in a food processor with olive oil. Strain and discard any solid residue. To prepare balsamic reduction, boil vinegar in a pot until reduced to a syrupy consistency, it will take about 15 minutes. To serve, slice remaining lobster half into 4 and lightly sear each slice in a hot pan. Place a seared lobster slice in the centre of the plate, cut a vine leaf parcel in half and stack next to the lobster. Garnish with salad. Drizzle over basil oil and balsamic reduction and sprinkle over cracked peppercorns. Serve with tomato salsa.

Harissa Beef Fillet with Chickpea Ragout & Cardamom Jus

Serves 4
Kilocalories 647 kcal > Protein 79 g > Carbohydrate 43 g > Total Fat 17 g

Harissa beef:
6 tsp cumin powder
6 tsp coriander powder
3 tsp caraway seeds
3 tsp chilli flakes
3 tsp chopped parsley
4 x 180 g (6 oz) beef fillets

Cardamom jus:
1 L (1¾ pt/4 cups) veal jus
4 tsp cardamom pods
salt and pepper to taste

Chickpea ragout:
5 tbsp olive oil
120 g (4¼ oz) onion, peeled and diced
20 g (¾ oz) garlic, peeled and chopped
200 g (7 oz) cooked chickpeas
120 g (4¼ oz) cooked broad beans
85 g (3 oz) sun-dried tomatoes, diced
4 sprigs of parsley to garnish

To prepare harissa, combine cumin, coriander, caraway seeds, chilli flakes and parsley. Transfer beef fillets to harissa and leave to marinate. Heat oil in a frying pan and sear beef over a high heat for 1 minute each side. Reduce heat to medium and continue cooking until beef is done to your liking. To prepare cardamom jus, place veal jus in a saucepan together with cardamom pods and boil until liquid has reduced to a syrupy consistency which coats the back of a spoon. Add seasoning. To prepare chickpea ragout, heat olive oil in a pan over a medium heat and sauté onion and garlic for 1–2 minutes, or until softened. Add chickpeas, broad beans and sun-dried tomatoes. Cook over a medium to low heat until tomatoes have softened. To serve, place chickpea ragout in the centre of 4 serving plates, place beef on top, spoon cardamom jus around beef, garnish with a sprig of parsley and serve.

Exotic Fruit Salad Flavoured with Light Jasmine Tea Syrup, Low-Fat Lime Yoghurt & Berries

Serves 4
Kilocalories 124 kcal > Protein 3 g > Carbohydrate 26 g > Total Fat 1 g

Fruit salad
120 g (4¼ oz) dragon fruit
120 g (4¼ oz) honeydew melon
120 g (4¼ oz) rock melon
120 g (4¼ oz) papaya
120 g (4¼ oz) pineapple
120 g (4¼ oz) strawberries
80 g (2¾ oz) kiwi fruit
160 g (5⅝ oz) lychees
80 g (2¾ oz) passionfruit (about 4)
40 g (1½ oz) mandarin oranges (about 8 segments)
80 g (2¾ oz) blueberries
80 g (2¾ oz) raspberries
40 g (1½ oz) physalis (Cape gooseberry) (about 8)

Light jasmine tea syrup:
2 jasmine tea bags
250 ml (9 fl oz/1 cup) boiling water
50 g (1¾ oz) sugar

Lime yoghurt:
8 tbsp low-fat yoghurt
6 tsp lime juice
1 tsp lime zest
4 sprigs mint leaves
8 tsp raspberry coulis

To prepare syrup, immerse jasmine tea bags in boiling water and leave to infuse for about 5 minutes. Remove and discard tea bags, then add sugar and stir until sugar is dissolved. Leave to cool completely. For fruit salad, cut dragon fruit, honeydew and rock melon, papaya, pineapple, strawberries and kiwi fruit into cubes. Peel lychees and remove seeds then halve, or quarter if large. Cut open passionfruit, scoop out pulp and seeds and reserve. Leaving the orange segments whole, remove as much of the white membrane as possible. Place all fruit in a large bowl and pour over cooled syrup. Gently mix and chill. To prepare lime yoghurt, mix yoghurt, lime juice, zest and mint leaves together. Spoon into 4 shot glasses and top with raspberry coulis. Serve alongside fruit salad.

Raspberry & Thyme Sorbet

Serves 4
Kilocalories 216 kcal > Protein 1 g > Carbohydrate 55 g > Total Fat 0 g

500 g (1 lb 2 oz) raspberry purée
250 ml (9 fl oz/1 cup) sugar syrup
leaves from 1 sprig thyme
juice from 1 lemon
small sprigs of thyme to garnish

Combine all ingredients and blend together
with a whisk. Freeze in an ice cream machine.
To serve, garnish with thyme. Keep remaining
sorbet frozen.

The Pan-Arabian Kitchen

COMMON FLAVOUR OF THE MIDDLE EAST

The vast expanse of the Middle East, spanning desert and coastline, encompasses an array of Arabian cultures that differ in both dialect and lifestyle. When it comes to the cuisine the differences are less obvious as, although dishes vary from country to country, what remain constant are the distinctive flavours that are recognizably pan-Arabian. Take for example the delicious salty taste of olives; grown across the Middle East they are unmistakably Arabian, add lemon to increase the distinctive flavour.

These recipes by Chef James Webster at Al Maha Desert Resort & Spa draw upon common ingredients that are used in pan-Arabian dishes. For example, sumac powder is sprinkled over meat and rice dishes, when mixed with wild thyme it makes zata, a common flavouring throughout the Middle East. Haloumi cheese, originating from Lebanon, has spread into the kitchens across the Middle East, its strong salty taste and hardy texture make it a great cooking cheese, or can be simply grilled as it is here.

Tian of Crab & Avocado

Serves 4
Kilocalories 197 kcal > Protein 25 g > Carbohydrate 2 g > Total Fat 10 g

80 g (2¾ oz) crab claws, cooked
85 g (3 oz) ripe avocado, peeled
5 g (⅛ oz) black sesame seeds
4 tbsp lemon juice
5 g (⅛ oz) sumac powder
10 g (¼ oz) fresh coriander, chopped
325 g (11½ oz) fresh white crabmeat
60 g (2¼ oz) smoked salmon
35 g (1¼ oz) frisée lettuce
salt, pepper and sugar to taste
4 lemon wedges, to garnish

De-shell crab claws and reserve meat. Slice half the avocado into 4 wedges, toss them in black sesame seeds and set aside. To prepare dressing, mash the remaining avocado to a smooth purée and whisk with 3 tbsp of the lemon juice, sumac powder and coriander. Adjust seasoning to taste, adding a pinch of sugar if necessary. Next, season white crabmeat with remaining lemon juice, salt and pepper. Divide into 4 portions and press each one into a frame on the serving plates. Neatly top with a slice of smoked salmon. Garnish with avocado wedges, frisée lettuce, crab claws and lemon wedges. Serve dressing separately.

Grilled Haloumi Cheese with Okra, Tomato & Mint Salad

Serves 4
Kilocalories 449 kcal > Protein 28 g > Carbohydrate 5 g > Total Fat 35 g

Tomato sauce:
160 g (5⅝ oz) tomatoes
4 shallots, peeled and sliced
1 tbsp extra-virgin olive oil
175 g (6 oz) fresh okra

Salad:
180 g (6¼ oz) plum tomatoes, skinned
and finely sliced
4 shallots, peeled and finely sliced
40 g (1½ oz) black olives
15 g (½ oz) lamb's lettuce (mache)
10 g (¼ oz) mint leaves
1–2 tbsp extra-virgin olive oil
salt and pepper to taste
455 g (1 lb) haloumi cheese
large pinch sumac powder

To prepare tomato sauce, blanch and skin tomatoes, then roughly chop. Sauté sliced shallots in olive oil for about 2 minutes until softened, add tomatoes to the pan and cook until thickened to a sauce. Trim okra, blanch in salted boiling water and refresh immediately in iced water. Drain and add to prepared tomato sauce. To prepare salad, combine tomato with shallots, olives, lamb's lettuce and mint leaves. Dress with half the olive oil and season to taste. For each serving, chargrill 3 slices of haloumi cheese until browned. Place directly onto 4 serving plates, brush with remaining olive oil and dust with sumac powder. Garnish with salad and serve with okra in tomato sauce.

Chargrilled Asparagus with Sun-Blushed Tomatoes, Rocket, Balsamic & Pesto

Serves 4
Kilocalories 145 kcal > Protein 4 g > Carbohydrate 3 g > Total Fat 13 g

185 g (6½ oz) medium asparagus spears
2 tbsp olive oil
salt and pepper to taste
155 g (5½ oz) plum tomatoes
1 sprig basil, shredded

Pesto:
10 g (¼ oz) basil leaves, shredded
25 g (1 oz) olive oil
10 g (¼ oz) parmesan cheese
10 g (¼ oz) pine nuts
5 g (⅛ oz) garlic

Dressing:
25 g (1 oz) mayonnaise
15 g (½ oz) aged balsamic vinegar
salt and pepper to taste

Garnishing:
40 g (1½ oz) rocket leaves
50 g (1¾ oz) natural low-fat yoghurt

To prepare vegetables, first blanch asparagus in boiling water until tender. Remove from heat, sieve and refresh immediately in iced water. Drain and pat asparagus dry, then lightly toss in 1 tbsp olive oil and seasoning and chargrill until browned. Remove the eye of each tomato and cut into wedges. Place on a baking tray and gently toss in remaining olive oil, seasoning, and a little shredded basil. Place baking tray in oven and roast on a low heat—150°C (300°F)—for about 2 hours until soft and partly dried. As the tomatoes are roasting, periodically pour off any juices that accumulate. To prepare pesto, blend remaining basil leaves and pesto ingredients in a food processor and process until mixture is smooth. Combine dressing ingredients and season. Arrange asparagus spears decoratively on serving plates, and place roasted tomato wedges in between each spear. Garnish with rocket leaves, drizzle asparagus with dressing and yoghurt and serve.

Salmon, Leek & Lobster Terrine with Keta Caviar Dressing

Serves 4
Kilocalories 154 kcal > Protein 14 g > Carbohydrate 1 g > Total Fat 11 g

120 g (4¼ oz) smoked salmon slices
100 g (3½ oz) lobster meat
500 ml (18 fl oz/2 cups) court bouillon
40 g (1½ oz) leeks
35 g (1¼ oz) extra-virgin olive oil
20 g (¾ oz) lemon juice
20 g (¾ oz) balsamic vinegar
15 g (½ oz) keta caviar (salmon eggs)
10 g (¼ oz) chives, chopped
salt and pepper to taste

Line a terrine mould with smoked salmon slices and set aside. Poach lobster meat in a court bouillon and leave aside to cool slightly. Slice leeks and fry them gently in a little of the olive oil until tender but not coloured. Remove lobster meat from court bouillon, and while still slightly warm, season with a little lemon juice and press into lined terrine mould. Arrange leeks inside mould. Fold any loose ends of salmon over the contents of the terrine and cover with a lid that sits just inside the terrine. Place a heavy weight (for example, a can of food) on top of the lid and transfer terrine to the refrigerator, preferably overnight, to allow contents to firm. Once set, carefully remove terrine from mould and slice with a sharp knife. Place slices in centre of 4 serving plates and brush with olive oil. Dress with balsamic vinegar, keta caviar, chives, remaining olive oil, season to taste and serve.

Wheat-Free Carrot Cake

Serves 4
Kilocalories 351 kcal > Protein 9 g > Carbohydrate 37 g > Total Fat 19 g

Carrot cake:
55 g (2 oz) brown sugar
10 g (¼ oz) lemon (juice and zest)
2 tsp cinnamon powder
55 g (2 oz) sunflower oil
75 g (2⅝ oz) gluten-free flour
15 g (½ oz) gram flour
60 g (2¼ oz) carrots, peeled and grated
4 tsp water

Icing:
½ tsp orange zest
35 g (1¼ oz) icing sugar
1 tsp orange juice
35 g (1¼ oz) low-fat cream cheese

Garnishing:
15 g (½ oz) marzipan and 1 drop of
orange food colouring
10 g (¼ oz) raspberries
4 chocolate tuiles

Pre-heat oven to 180°C (360°F). Oil and line a baking tin with greaseproof paper and set aside. Beat together brown sugar, lemon juice and zest, cinnamon and oil until well blended. Mix in both flours, grated carrots and water. Pour into the prepared tin and bake for 15 minutes, or until a toothpick inserted in centre of the cake comes out clean. Leave cake in tin to cool slightly before turning out onto wire rack to cool completely. To prepare icing, add orange zest to icing sugar and mix in just enough juice and cream cheese to create a thick icing. Spread over top of cooled cake. Fashion baby carrots from marzipan, using a drop of orange colouring. Garnish cake with marzipan carrots, raspberries, chocolate tuiles and serve.

Spa Digest

The Middle East covers a wide range of terrain and landscapes, from jaw-dropping mountain ranges to seemingly never-ending desert, from seaside destinations to bustling cities. The possibilities are limitless and spa-goers can choose their holiday to suit any combination of tastes. All the mystery and romanticism of exotic Arabia flavour the growing number of spas in the region, which draw therapies from the Middle East itself as well as from Eastern and Western traditions.

Many of the spas featured here offer authentic hammam rituals or Cleopatra-style treatments and other Arabian healing therapies, that ensure a truly memorable spa break. These time-honoured traditions are commonly accompanied by newer spa therapies that come from around the world, such as colour and crystal healing, body massages, wraps and scrubs, and various thalassotherapy techniques. Whether it's to be an opulent hotel in Dubai, a desert eco-resort, or by the Dead Sea, the Spa Digest introduces you to the region's best and most stylish spas. Whichever you choose, Arabia is the perfect setting for a well-deserved indulgence.

The Spa & Wellness Centre, Four Seasons Hotel Cairo at The First Residence

CAIRO, EGYPT

With a magical view of Egypt's ancient pyramids and the River Nile, guests can escape to a welcoming and authentic Arabian sanctuary. Whether your feet are tired from taking in the nearby ancient sites, or from hours of shopping at the haute couture boutiques and galleries of the First Residence complex, Four Seasons Hotel Cairo at The First Residence's Spa & Wellness Centre will certainly help to ease away any tension.

At the spa's entrance, the sense of Arabian opulence is immediately apparent with traditional details sitting comfortably alongside modern spa conveniences. Beauty was of great importance to the ancient Egyptians. They are known for pampering their bodies with creams and oils and their desire for cleanliness and hygiene provided a basis for beautifying rituals. Beauty, according to traditional Egyptian philosophy, embraces both the inner and outer self. Befittingly, you will find this holistic approach in all of the treatments.

Once prepared and ready to choose from the menu, you will find a gamut of treatments to pamper the whole body. The Papyrus Wrap is one example. In ancient times, the Egyptians encouraged skin rejuvenation by wrapping themselves in oils and linen. Following this tradition, the Papyrus Wrap treatment involves a ritual application of honey and herbs that soothes and nourishes the skin.

Marrying both ancient knowledge of natural ingredients and modern facial treatments, the Spa & Wellness Centre offers treatments that both revive the skin and guard against premature ageing. The Nefertiti Facial is an age-old treatment that softens and moisturizes the skin, promoting cell renewal. Princesses in the royal palaces of Ancient Egypt would be taught how to prepare it for their own use. In the spa, guests can lie back and relax as a purée of flowers is applied to the face, and aromatic oils fill the room with sweet intoxication. A fine mist of rosewater adds a gentle finish to this blissful

facial treatment that leaves you looking and feeling just like a princess. Other facials inspired by the ancient world include the King Tut Facial and the Egyptian coffee mask.

Those in need of a massage, should try the divine Imperial Massage. Two therapists are on hand to massage the whole body in complete synchrony. By using a combination of long sensuous strokes and muscle manipulation with aromatic oils, the body is completely relaxed and renewed by the end of the 30-minute treatment. Besides this, the spa's comprehensive list of massages includes many from Asia such as the Javanese lulur, the traditional Thai massage and the ayurvedic shirodhara therapy.

Designed exclusively for this Spa & Wellness Centre is a series of treatments using the unique therapeutic ingredients from the Dead Sea in Jordan. One example is the Exfoliating Salt Scrub. First, a refreshing application of Dead Sea water is poured onto the body, followed by a mixture of exfoliating salts to cleanse, rejuvenate and soften the skin.

The Spa & Wellness Centre also caters to those who prefer their personal space. Guests can enjoy their own private spa for three hours; the experience comes complete with a private sauna, whirlpool and shower. The package continues with a relaxing pharaonic massage fit for royalty with Egyptian aromatic oils specifically chosen for each individual. A heated poultice of aromatic herbs is then used to soothe your tired muscles and nourish the skin as you rest your gaze on the view of the Nile.

THIS PAGE (FROM LEFT): Highly skilled and experienced spa therapists work in tandem to create a massage experience not easily forgotten; the hydrotherapy bath crystals relax and stimulate the mind and body with their rejuvenating blend of eucalyptus, peppermint, grapefruit and lavender.
OPPOSITE (FROM LEFT): The main outdoor pool on the fourth floor is ideal for catching up with some exercise or basking in the sunshine; encapsulating the beauty of Arabia, the spa is a tranquil space for some first-class pampring.

Spa Statistics

TYPE OF SPA
Hotel Spa

SPA AREA
900 sq m (9,700 sq ft)

FACILITIES
8 single treatment rooms, 1 double treatment room; 2 relaxation lounges; 1 whirlpool, 1 plunge pool; 1 sauna, 1 steam room (in both the men's and women's areas), 2 aromatherapy steam rooms; hair salon, nail salon, beauty salon; 1 fitness facility and private ladies-only workout room; rooftop pool, children's pool

SIGNATURE TREATMENTS
Papyrus Wrap, Nefertiti Facial, Exfoliating Salt Scrub and Imperial Massage

OTHER TREATMENTS AND THERAPIES
Aromatherapy, ayurveda, baths, body scrubs, body wraps, facial treatments, hair and scalp treatments, hand and foot treatments, hot stone therapies, hydrotherapy, Indonesian therapies, manicures/pedicures, massages, Thai therapies, waxing

PROVISIONS FOR COUPLES
An intimate private 'spa-within-a-spa' offers a separate Jacuzzi, sauna and shower exclusively for couples.

SPA CUISINE
Health drinks, mineral water and fresh apples are available. Decaffeinated coffee and tea are served every morning from 6.00 am to 10.00 am.

SERVICES
Personal trainer

LANGUAGES SPOKEN BY THERAPISTS
English, Arabic

ADMISSION
Exclusively for hotel guests

CONTACT
The First Residence
35 Giza Street
Giza, Cairo
Egypt 12311
T +20 2 573 1212
F +20 2 568 1616
E nada.ismail@fourseasons.com
W www.fourseasons.com

Four Seasons Hotel Cairo at Nile Plaza

CAIRO, EGYPT

This is a calm and peaceful sanctuary that lies in the heart of bustling Cairo. Make your way to the fifth floor of the 30-storey Four Seasons Hotel Cairo at Nile Plaza and you will find the entire floor dedicated to beauty, well-being and leisure. The unique Daniela Steiner Beauty & Wellness Centre is the largest full-service spa in Cairo. Tranquillity greets you with the glow of candles, coupled with soft music emanating from the spa's 15 treatment rooms for men and women, including a couple's suite. Its lush décor is a medley of creams and beige tones.

Within this serene retreat, each spa treatment renews the balance of body, mind and soul. Ancient purifying rituals from the Middle East, Asia and Europe, are applied with an expert touch by the skilled beauty and massage specialists.

One such body treatment is the spa's Pharaonic Massage, inspired by the cultures and traditions of the Middle East. Once reserved for Egyptian royalty, this massage uses aromatic poultices filled with fresh camomile and mint, which have been dipped in the warm essential oils of jasmine and rose.

THIS PAGE (FROM LEFT): The Daniela Steiner Beauty & Wellness Spa provides an ultimate hideaway, guests can relax in this spacious wet area before the treatment begins; the spa has 15 treatment rooms that cater for men and women, including one couple's suite, this single treatment room comes complete with private shower. OPPOSITE (FROM TOP): Guests can sit back and take in an uninterrupted view of the Nile in total comfort; an alternative to spa therapy is a workout at the hotel's superb 24-hour gymnasium to ensure complete well-being.

Whether you choose a 50-minute massage, or an 80-minute one, tired muscles will be soothed, the skin nourished, and the body completely relaxed. Romantic fantasies of bathing in a pool of milk and honey are met at the Daniela Steiner Spa. Indulge in a Cleopatra Treatment and feel like the famed queen herself as you soak in the enriching milk and honey bath with the essential oil of rosemary that will soothe, condition and soften the skin. A relaxing body massage with sweet almond oil then follows.

The Swiss-made spa products used here are made with only the highest quality and the most natural essences of flowers, fruits, seeds, shoots, shells and leaves, each offering the active ingredients that give radiant and beautiful skin.

For those looking for relaxation alfresco, the spa leads to an extensive rooftop terrace, overlooking the Nile and its lush greenery. Here, high above the streets of Cairo, are three heated pools, one indoor pool, and 17 poolside cabanas with private, shaded seating areas and individual washrooms.

Once renewed and energized, venture out to explore Cairo's rich history and cosmopolitan spirit. The hotel sits right on the banks of the legendary Nile River. Located in Cairo's Garden City district, the hotel is surrounded by vestiges of another era; the grand Belle Epoque and Art Deco mansions. Further beyond lie the ancient treasures that are a must-see for any visitor to Egypt.

Spa Statistics

TYPE OF SPA
Hotel Spa

SPA AREA
1,750 sq m (18,800 sq ft)

FACILITIES
14 single treatment rooms, 1 double treatment room; 1 Jacuzzi, 2 plunge pools, 1 whirlpool; 2 saunas, 2 steam rooms; 24-hour gymnasium; 3 outdoor swimming pools with private poolside cabanas, 1 indoor swimming pool

SIGNATURE TREATMENTS
Cleopatra's Treatment, Pharaonic Massage, Volcanic Clay

OTHER TREATMENTS AND THERAPIES
Anti-cellulite treatments, aromatherapy, body cleansing, body scrubs, body wraps, facial treatments, firming and slimming treatments, manicures/pedicures, massages reflexology

PROVISIONS FOR COUPLES
Special skincare treatment for two; 1 double treatment room

SPA CUISINE
Refreshments and light meals can be ordered from the Pool Grill.

ACTIVITIES AND PROGRAMMES
Personal trainers are available 24-hours a day.

LANGUAGES SPOKEN BY THERAPISTS
English, Arabic, Balinese, German, Italian and Russian

ADMISSION
Exclusively for hotel guests. Visiting guests can use the spa for treatments and therapies only.

CONTACT
Four Seasons Hotel Cairo at Nile Plaza
1089 Corniche El Nil
P.O. Box 63 Maglis El Shaab
Garden City, Cairo
Egypt 11519
T +20 2 791 7000
F +20 2 791 6900
E reservations.cai@fourseasons.com
W www.fourseasons.com

Four Seasons Resort Sharm El Sheikh

SINAI, EGYPT

At 510 square metres (5,500 square feet), Four Seasons Resort Sharm El Sheikh is the largest and most luxurious beauty and wellness spa in the region with both indoor and outdoor treatment areas. The courtyard fountains and luscious gardens splashed with colours and swaying palm trees, provide many quiet spots to relax and wonder. Set against the stark beauty of the desert, this hillside resort overlooks the shimmering Gulf of Aqaba, and guests can feel the warm breeze from the Red Sea in the private open-air massage rooms

Inside are 13 treatment rooms, a steam room and sauna and—as privacy is paramount—entirely separate facilities for men and women. For those wanting to share the experience with their partner, double treatment rooms are also available.

The spa offers an extensive menu of all-natural treatments by Daniela Steiner. Each beauty programme is personalized and created for the special needs of each client—the type of massage, the length of the treatment, the kind of body wrap and the combination of substances—and the sole purpose is rejuvenation, relaxation and renewal.

An interesting treatment offered at the Beauty and Wellness Spa is the Cleopatra Bath. This three-hour session is a combination of the Bedouin Treatment, Lotus Bath and Classic Facial treatment. For centuries, nomadic Bedouin tribes of Sinai have

survived in the harsh desert. Inspired by their traditions, the Bedouin Treatment begins with a Sahara sand scrub to energize and lift the spirits. This is followed by a soothing massage with aromatic essential oils. The relaxing journey continues with a luxurious Lotus Bath that will pique the senses. A floating array of colourful petals of exotic flowers pleases the eye, while their wonderful heady aromas fill the bath. Not forgetting the most visible part of your body—your face—this indulgent treatment ends with a Classic Facial. This includes a deep cleanse, eyebrow shaping, and a regenerating massage. The ingredients used are a combination of top-quality extracts sourced from nature itself. Flowers, fruits, seeds, shoots, shells and leaves are processed to supply oils and waxes containing active ingredients.

For those seeking more vigorous activities, Sharm El Sheikh is one of the world's most accessible resort destinations for snorkelling and scuba-diving. The Ras Muhammed National Park features 90 metres (295 feet) of vertical reefs, the natural habitat of a multitude of marine life that is unique to the area. Landlubbers and history buffs may prefer to venture to the many fascinating sites near the resort. Whether in a caravan of camels or a jeep safari, you can visit the desert villages of the nomadic Bedouin, or catch the sunrise over St Catherine's Monastery and Mount Sinai. Whatever you choose, unwinding at the Four Seasons Resort Sharm El Sheikh is easy.

THIS PAGE: **Fountains and courtyards reflect the resort's luxurious Middle-Eastern style.**
OPPOSITE (CLOCKWISE FROM LEFT): **The Waha pool is perfect for sunbathers and serves as a great relaxing spot; 100 per cent natural ingredients are used in the spa treatments; couples can enjoy their spa experience together in the double treatment rooms and private courtyard that offer an oasis of calm and privacy.**

Spa Statistics

TYPE OF SPA
Resort Spa

SPA AREA
510 sq m (5,500 sq ft)

FACILITIES
8 indoor single treatment rooms, 4 outdoor treatment rooms, 1 double treatment room; 3 relaxation lounges; 2 outdoor whirlpools; 2 steam rooms, 4 saunas; 1 beauty salon; 1 gymnasium; 1 lap pool, 2 outdoor swimming pools, 2 children's playpools, kid's club

SIGNATURE TREATMENTS
Bedouin Treatment, Cleopatra Treatments, Pharaonic Massage

OTHER TREATMENTS AND THERAPIES
After-sun treatment, anti-ageing treatment, aromatherapy, baths, body scrubs, body wraps, facial treatments, firming and slimming treatments, massages, reflexology, salon services, Thai massage

SPA CUISINE
Healthy, light and low-fat cuisine featuring Middle Eastern food is available at the pool restaurant. Lebanese and Italian cuisine are available at the resort's restaurants.

SERVICES
Diving equipment rental, diving lessons

LANGUAGES SPOKEN BY THERAPISTS
English, Arabic, German, Italian, Thai

ADMISSION
Exclusively for resort guests

CONTACT
Four Seasons Resort Sharm El Sheikh
One Four Seasons Boulevard
P.O. Box 203
Sharm El Sheikh, South Sinai
Egypt
T +2069 3 603 555
F +2069 3 603 550
E daniela.steiner@fourseasons.com
W www.fourseasons.com

Hyatt Regency Sharm El Sheikh

SINAI, EGYPT

Hyatt Regency at Sharm El Sheikh is a place 'where the people go to play'. And no wonder too, as within the 35 hectares (86½ acres) of the resort lies unlimited and diverse leisure pursuits at the Club Olympus—home to a complete indoor gym and aerobics studio, and an extensive spa area.

Step through the elegant green and white marble entrance of Club Olympus and immediately, the feeling of peace and tranquillity envelops. Within the magnificent Moorish-style men's and women's spas, the walls are decorated with thousands of sparkling jewel-toned tiles. Here is a sanctuary from the hurly burly of everyday life, a place for complete relaxation and utter indulgence.

Enjoy a languorous poolside massage or relax in the sauna, steam room or cold plunge pool. Within the five spacious treatment rooms, or seafront tent, luxurious pampering will harmonize the body, mind and spirit. Whether to reduce tension, improve circulation, eliminate soreness or for an overall sense of well-being, the massages offered at the spa are all customized and designed for individual needs.

Service is of the essence here too. Guests can choose to experience a particular type of massage or an integrated one. Treatment can be tailor-made;

not only are the massage oils carefully-selected and hand-blended, guests can even choose their own scented oils for certain massages too. For example, the Luxury Aromatherapy Massage is a full body treatment beginning with skin brushing and cleansing. This is followed by an aromatherapy massage using essential oils—which are known for their purity and potency—chosen specifically for the guest's requirements. These oils and massage combined, leave the body totally relaxed.

Another must-try is the Hyatt Nature Scrub which is made with Egypt's finest natural ingredients. It is an extraordinary combination of fresh fruits, coconut, coffee, oil and sugar cane crystals—all good enough to eat. This delicious mixture is applied onto the skin, gently buffing away ageing skin cells. The alpha hydroxyl agents in the honey, combined with the fruits and other essential ingredients, gently remove dirt and toxins from the skin's outer layer, encouraging healthy blood flow to the skin's surface. The result is beautifully soft, smooth and radiant skin.

Taking advantage of the healing properties of the region's resources is the Black Nile Mud Scrub. Organic black River Nile mud improves skin texture

and extracts pore-clogging impurities that damage and weaken skin. This rare mud contains 49 per cent humic acid (from the class of hydroxyl acids) vitamins A, B1, B2, B12 and trace minerals. The mud is applied to the arms, legs, back and stomach. Guests are then wrapped in towels for around 15 to 20 minutes. During this time, a relaxing scalp and facial massage is administered. After resting, warm towels are applied to wipe away the mud, leaving the skin soft and rejuvenated.

After an activity-filled day out on the beach, diving amongst the coral reefs, or out on an expedition to the ancient biblical sites nearby, the spa is indeed the perfect place for guests to restore and renew body, mind and spirit.

THIS PAGE (FROM TOP): The distinctive style of Arabia combines with the holistic approach in this haven of well-being; sitting right by the Red Sea, the spa offers many alternative locations for treatment.
OPPOSITE (FROM TOP): A tailor-made massage at the spa ensures a renewed spirit; the spa pool offers sunshine and cool respite from the heat.

Spa Statistics

TYPE OF SPA
Resort Spa

SPA AREA
500 sq m (5,380 sq ft)

FACILITIES
5 single treatment rooms, 1 seafront treatment tent; 1 Jacuzzi; 1 sauna, 1 steam room, steam cabinet; 1 indoor gymnasium, 4 floodlit tennis courts, 1 floodlit exhibition court, 2 air-conditioned squash courts

SIGNATURE TREATMENTS
Black Nile Mud Scrub, South Sinai Massage, Deluxe Facial

OTHER TREATMENTS AND THERAPIES
After-sun treatments, anti-cellulite treatments, aromatherapy, body scrubs, facial treatments, hair and scalp treatments, hand and foot treatments, hot stone therapies, Indonesian therapies, massages, Thai therapies

ACTIVITIES AND PROGRAMMES
Abdominal classes, aerobics, aqua toning, meditation, pilates

SERVICES
Oasis Kids Club, personal training

LANGUAGES SPOKEN BY THERAPISTS
English, Arabic

ADMISSION
Open to staying and non-staying guests

CONTACT
Hyatt Regency Sharm El Sheikh
The Gardens Bay, P.O Box 58
Sharm El Sheikh, South Sinai
Egypt
T +20 69 360 1234
F +20 69 360 3600
E sharm@hyattintl.com
W www.sharm.hyatt.com

Zara Spa at the Mövenpick Resort & Spa

DEAD SEA, JORDAN

For some the Dead Sea was considered a gift from the gods, and a place where man could heal, unwind and relax. At the Mövenpick Resort & Spa Dead Sea, it is easy to believe. This five-star resort is located on the northeastern shore of the historic Dead Sea—the lowest point on earth at 400 metres (1,312 feet) below sea level, and the resort's stunning natural surroundings, accompanied by year-round filtered sunshine, are just an introduction to this world of wellness and healing.

Zara Spa opened in May 1999. At 6,000 square metres (64,583 square feet), it is one of the largest and most prestigious spas in the region, and is dedicated to pampering the senses and bringing harmony between body and soul. Much like the Mövenpick Hotels & Resorts group, the spa's international renown has improved year on year and was named Best Spa in the region in the Middle East and North Africa Travel Awards 2005.

Zara Spa's mission is to provide a haven of relaxation, a chance to get away from the stress of everyday life. That is why everything in the spa is geared towards an ambience of complete serenity, relaxation and luxuriant pampering. At first glance, this philosophy is revealed in its architecture, which is in itself reminiscent of an age of luxury. It stylishly complements the surrounding resort complex, with its close-to-nature and understated manner. Most of its guest rooms feature a multifaceted village design of traditional stone construction, evoking all the exoticism of Arabia.

The Middle Eastern theme continues throughout Zara Spa. Beneath the beautiful mosaic domes of the Eastern-inspired Thermarium and Turkish hammam, guests can take in the atmosphere before they proceed to their treatments. The Thermarium includes a caldarium (warm steam room), laconium (hot dry room), mint-scented tropical rain showers,

soap massage rooms and indoor and outdoor rest areas. Here, heat and water are used together to open the pores, increase circulation and stimulate the lymphatic system; the area is the perfect place to prepare for the spa's body and facial treatments.

Taking advantage of the close proximity to the Dead Sea and its natural healing properties, Zara Spa offers a gamut of pools with varying levels of salt concentration, and each comes with its own unique features and benefits. The relaxing heated hydropool, with a 3 per cent salt concentration, stimulates blood circulation and massages tired and tense muscles with its advanced pressure jets that are carefully aimed across the whole of the body.

In the pool area of the spa, arched windows frame amazing views of the Dead Sea, enhancing the luxurious experience. The first Dead Sea Pool is heated to a constant 36°C (97°F) and guests can lie back and relax while the water and heat work together to loosen the body. The second Dead Sea Pool, on the other hand, contains pure Dead Sea water with a salt concentration of 28–33 per cent. The various minerals and nutrients in the Dead Sea saltwater—including magnesium, potassium and calcium chloride—are known for their healing properties that help to eliminate toxins in the body, boost the immune system and balance the body's pH

levels. The salt may sting but any cuts or skin abrasions will heal quickly and the water is even believed to help skin ailments such as eczema. It is encouraged that people spend 10 minutes in the salt pool five times per day, in order to receive the full benefits of the saltwater.

The hydrotherapy offered by the spa extends to its reflexology-inspired pool. Guests may walk along the water jets in the Kneipp foot massage pool, to stimulate the pressure points in the feet and increase circulation, after which a soak in the hydropool with its massaging jets will complete the full body water massage.

The body treatments on Zara Spa's menu offer a sensory experience and use international skincare products alongside 100 per cent natural and nutrient-rich Dead Sea mud and salt. Guests can choose from the Hydro Experience, Alternative Therapy, Facial and Skin, Body Slimming and Firming, Hands and Feet, Dead Sea Body, Massage and Dry Flotation menus.

A must-try treatment from the Dry Flotation menu is the 55-minute-long Dead Sea Natural Mud Wrap and Dry Float. Soothing music plays overhead as the body is cocooned in a pure Dead Sea mud wrap. Proven to have therapeutic properties that relieve muscle tension and nourish dry skin, this

THIS PAGE (FROM TOP): Arabian village style emanates throughout the resort; the hydropool looking out onto the Dead Sea.
OPPOSITE (CLOCKWISE FROM TOP): Sunset over the Dead Sea provides an amazing backdrop to the resort; the caldarium, or warm steam room, offers cool respite to the hammam and laconium; the stunning hydropool where hidden massage jets pummel the body.

unique mud is used for its high content of silicates—a much sought-after, special ingredient that tightens the skin. This firming and toning effect means the mud is highly recommended for new mothers wishing to regain their figures and for anyone in search of weight loss. The mud also works to improve body texture and minimize wrinkles. Once the body is prepared and wrapped, guests can lie back and unwind on the dry flotation bed. As the bed melts away and the body is seemingly suspended, an aromatic face and scalp massage is performed simultaneously. This superb treatment is guaranteed to ease the body into a deep relaxation. In fact, it is so relaxing, it's said that one flotation session equates to a full night's sleep.

From the Hydro Experience menu, the Four Hand Massage is administered simultaneously with

the Affusion Shower. Just as the name implies, two therapists perform a manual massage with almond oil in complete synchrony while the aromatic rain droplets fall onto the body, doubling the benefits of this soothing massage. The Dead Sea water used in the shower is heated to body temperature to ensure maximum effect. This treatment is known to improve circulation and lymphatic flow, which aid the body in cleansing itself of toxins. Before leaving the spa, guests must try the signature Dead Sea Salt Scrub. The exfoliating salt is extremely effective and the skin will feel the softest it has ever felt. What's more, for those seeking total privacy, Zara Spa offers exclusive Royal Therapy Suites.

Day-trips from the resort include Jordan's capital Amman, just a 40-minute drive away. The busy souks and local cuisine will tantalize any traveller's taste. Alternatively, if a bustling city does not appeal, the ancient religious site of Mount Nebo is also just under an hour's car ride away. For a real Arabian experience, visitors should take a three-hour drive south towards the ancient Nabataean traders' city of Petra. This stunning city is carved out of vibrant red rock and is where *Indiana Jones* was filmed. Nearby is Wadi Rum, the desert valley where *Lawrence of Arabia* was set.

On your return, the freshwater infinity-edge pool provides a refreshing change from the saltwater pools. From here, guests can enjoy an endless perspective of the surrounding view. On the poolside, light refreshments are served at the terrace—the ideal location to watch spectacular sunsets over the Dead Sea. With a drink in hand and the breathtaking scenery surrounding you, no wonder they call this 'a world of pure indulgence'.

Spa Statistics

TYPE OF SPA
Resort Spa

SPA AREA
6,000 sq m (64,580 sq ft)

FACILITIES
22 treatment rooms; relaxation areas for both men and women, lounge with Japanese massage chairs; Kneipp foot treading pool, 1 outdoor heated hydropool, indoor Dead Sea pool, Dead Sea whirlpool, tropical rain and fog showers; 1 flotation bed; male and female Thermarium, male and female Turkish hammam; manicure and pedicure room; gymnasium, aerobics studio; 1 freshwater swimming pool; tennis courts

SIGNATURE TREATMENTS
Dead Sea Natural Mud Wrap and Dry Float, Four Hands Massage in the Affusion Shower, Dead Sea Salt Scrub

OTHER TREATMENTS AND THERAPIES
Acupuncture, body scrubs, body wraps, Dead Sea facial treatments, dry flotation treatments, facial treatments, firming and slimming treatments, hand and foot treatments, hot stone therapies, manicures/pedicures, massages, reflexology, specialized facial treatments, thalassotherapy, Thalgo facial treatments

SERVICES
The Therapy Centre uses the unique natural resources of the Dead Sea, climate, sea water and mud to treat skin diseases, rheuma and psoriatic arthritis, and joint problems. There is also an in-house dermatologist, and a specialist in physical medicine, resort medicine and rehabilitation.

LANGUAGES SPOKEN BY THERAPISTS
English, Arabic

ADMISSION
Open to staying and non-staying guests

CONTACT
Mövenpick Resort & Spa Dead Sea
P.O. Box 815538
11180 Amman
Jordan
T +962 5 356 1111
F +962 5 356 1125
E zaraspa@movenpick-deadsea.com
W www.zaraspa.com

Jordan Valley Marriott Resort & Spa

DEAD SEA, JORDAN

Four hundred metres (1,312 feet) below sea level, at the lowest point on earth, lies the Jordan Valley Marriott Resort & Spa. Ideally located, it is set along the mineral-rich Dead Sea, which has long been revered for its healing powers since ancient times. Naturally, this spa aims to offer guests the best in relaxation and rejuvenation.

The breathtaking location of Jordan Valley Marriott Resort & Spa is in itself unique. Situated at the northern end of the Dead Sea, the typical Mediterranean climate of mild winters and hot summers provides the perfect conditions for a spa break. The unpolluted air is pollen-free all year round and the special climatic conditions of the region and tranquillity of the surrounding desert induce an overall feeling of total well-being. What's more, the low altitude enriches the air with oxygen— there is 10 per cent more here than at sea level. Visitors to the area will also find an increase in their body's metabolic activity as the low level of humidity, combined with the fast evaporation rate of the Dead Sea water, works its magic.

At the 3,000-square-metre (32,291-square-foot) spa, there are eight individual treatment rooms, and eight massage and facial treatment rooms. Each is a sanctuary where exquisite treatments—that have been carefully designed to incorporate the natural and unique elements of the Dead Sea—are expertly administered. Research has shown that when soaking in the waters of the Dead Sea, the salt and minerals work together to draw toxins through the pores of the body. The Jordan Valley Marriott Resort & Spa has a Dead Sea salt pool that uses water from the Dead Sea with a salt concentration of 35 per cent. A soak in this pool will beautify, purify, cleanse, heal and nourish the body.

The treatments at the spa are combined with luxury spa products, and guests can expect both

Spa Statistics

TYPE OF SPA
Resort Spa

SPA AREA
3,000 sq m (32,291 sq ft)

FACILITIES
8 single treatment rooms, 8 massage and facial treatment rooms; 1 relaxation area; 5 hydrotherapy areas, 4 whirlpools; 2 saunas, 2 steam rooms, hammam; cardio studio, gymnasium; 3 swimming pools (Dead Sea salt pool, fresh water pool and spa pool); 1 tennis court, kid's pool and entertainment area

SIGNATURE TREATMENTS
Dead Sea Salt Scrub, Dead Sea Mud Wrap, Facial Mask, Milk and Honey Wrap

OTHER TREATMENTS AND THERAPIES
Body scrubs, body wraps, facial treatments, hot stone therapies, hydrotherapy, massages

SERVICES
Fitness consultations

LANGUAGES SPOKEN BY THERAPISTS
English, Arabic

ADMISSION
Open to staying and non-staying guests

CONTACT
Jordan Valley Marriott Resort & Spa
P.O Box 928417
11190 Amman
Jordan
T +962 5 356 0400
   +962 6 569 9936 (reservations)
F +962 5 356 0444
E jordanvalley@marriotthotels.com
W www.marriott.com

heat and cooling treatments to cleanse and relax the body. One signature treatment is a full body experience where the skin is scrubbed and exfoliated with a loofah and, of course, natural Dead Sea salts. The body is then swathed in healing Dead Sea mud that draws impurities, completely renewing the skin.

Besides treatments, guests can relax in the warmth of the hammam or sauna. There is also the Dead Sea rock steam room to help improve the body's circulation. For those looking for a purely Middle Eastern spa experience, the Turkish baths are just the thing. The steam is infused with aromatherapy essences and herbal extracts which work to enhance the skin's complexion. After all that heat, choose to cool down in either the indoor freshwater pool or relax and float in the Dead Sea salt pool. Alternatively, try the spa pool which incorporates a variety of body jets and nourishing mineral-rich water that has been set at the optimal temperature so that the body can rebalance. After a rejuvenating treatment at the spa, round up the wellness experience with a light and healthy meal at one of the resort's restaurants.

For more active guests, there is a choice of activities, from beach volleyball to tennis and jogging. Alternatively, the location is so rich in history, excursions are aplenty, from the Christian Baptist site and the Church of Mosaics, to the seaside resort of Aqaba, there is ample choice for a great day out.

THIS PAGE: The calming sand and beige tones of the spa's lobby area.
OPPOSITE (CLOCKWISE FROM TOP): Hot stone therapies are just one of the cosmopolitan treatments available at the spa; guests can enjoy all the goodness of the Dead Sea in the spa's very own Dead Sea salt pool; one of the outdoor pools with views of the Dead Sea beyond.

Grand Hills Hotel & Spa

BROUMANA, LEBANON

Amid fresh pines, high up in the hilly landscape 750 metres (2,460 feet) above sea level, lies the Grand Hills Hotel & Spa. The resort is located at the gateway of Lebanon's popular mountain village, Broumana, where the weather is cooler. Among the luscious greenery and breathtaking coastal and mountain views, it is a perfect natural retreat.

Inside, the spa awaits. Its charming Asian atmosphere permeates and the spa menu draws its holistic therapies from ancient Chinese techniques. The spa's philosophy is guided by the five elements—water, fire, wind, metal and earth—which help to identify and treat specific problems. The idea of traditional Chinese medicine (TCM) is to restore the balance between yin and yang and to encourage the healthy flow of chi throughout the whole body.

The spa successfully combines tradition with modern spa techniques. For instance, the ancient Chinese method of healing mixes with the innovative Swiss technology of Chromatherapy—a colour, light and energy motion technique that is used to achieve toned and firmer skin. Plant therapy is also used for deep body cleansing, which encourages the gradual recovery and improvement of the physique.

A must-try at the spa is the Balneo Therapy. Guests can lie back and relax while being massaged in a tub of bubbling water. This hydro-massage treatment uses lyophilized (freeze-dried) sea water, algae from the Atlantic Ocean, and Dead Sea salts each with effective toning, rebalancing and rejuvenating essential oils.

Other highly beneficial therapies are available from the range of Body Treatments. Each involves a clay body mask followed by an essential oil massage. Both techniques can be used to slim, tone and relax, as well as to rid any water retention. The Body Treatments are based on TCM, but they also use the more modern technique of lymphatic drainage

massage. The deep tissue massage encourages the lymphatic circulation which in turn expels toxins and reduces water retention. This fusion of ancient therapies and new techniques is complemented by the spa products from the highly reputable international Swiss brand, Phytobiodermie.

Another traditional treatment is acupuncture. This ancient method entails needles being pierced at strategic points along the body's paths of energy or meridian points. Vital energy, or chi, circulates through these channels and it's believed that illness occurs when there is a blockage or imbalance of chi. Acupuncture, along with various herbs, is used to restore balance in the body.

The spa also has separate saunas, Jacuzzis and steam rooms for men and women. The Tonic Gym serves fitness fanatics with four floors of exercise options. The complex contains a gymnasium, squash courts and fitness, aerobics and ballet rooms. The Tonic Gym boasts tennis courts and jogging and bicycle lanes that are situated outside in the grounds. Given this haven of luxury with five-star settings, complete relaxation, rejuvenation and a completely energized body are guaranteed.

THIS PAGE (FROM LEFT): High up in the hilltop, the resort's path is a welcoming sight; reminders of exotic Arabia are present in the décor throughout Grand Hills. OPPOSITE (CLOCKWISE FROM TOP): Nestled among the trees, the swimming pool is the perfect place to take in the refreshing mountain air; the resort features stunning landscaped gardens promising complete relaxation; making good use of the surroundings, guests can unwind in the Jacuzzi while enjoying the view.

Spa Statistics

TYPE OF SPA
Hotel Mountain Spa

SPA AREA
2,978 sq m (32,054 sq ft)

FACILITIES
22 single indoor treatment rooms, 4 double indoor treatment rooms; 2 saunas, 2 steam baths, 1 hammam; gymnasium; 1 indoor and 1 outdoor swimming pool; hair salon

SIGNATURE TREATMENTS
Balneo Therapy, Body Peeling, Body and Facial Care with Chromatherapy and Essential Oils

OTHER TREATMENTS AND THERAPIES
Acupuncture, aromatherapy, Chinese therapies, facial treatments, firming and slimming treatments, hand and foot treatments, make-up services, osteopathy, reflexology, reiki, Thai therapies, thalassotherapy

ACTIVITIES AND PROGRAMMES
Aerobics, make-up classes, tae-bo, tae-kwon-do, tattooing

SERVICES
Bride and groom package, tailor-made packages

LANGUAGES SPOKEN BY THERAPISTS
English, Arabic

ADMISSION
Open to staying and non-staying guests

CONTACT
Grand Hills Hotel & Spa
Al Charkiah Road
Broumana
Lebanon
T +961 4 862 888
F +961 4 861 888
E info@grandhillsvillage.com
W www.grandhillsvillage.com

The Spa at the Chedi

MUSCAT, SULTANATE OF OMAN

Sophisticated, elegant, luxurious. Three words that sum up The Chedi Muscat. Located at the foot of the glorious Hajjar mountain range, on the shores of the Boushar beachfront in Oman, this is the perfect setting for restoring and revitalizing the spirit.

Muscat, Oman's capital, is often described as the 'Jewel of Arabia'. Colonized by the Portuguese in the 16th century, the city became an indispensable trading post between the Orient and the Western world. Today, the city is abuzz with its unique and intriguing ambience and all around, tradition is combined with modern style and innovation.

These contrasts of old and new, East and West, are brilliantly displayed at The Spa at The Chedi. Its Omani architecture of curved and pointed arches, high narrow windows, domes and gleaming white façades is juxtaposed with clean modern and minimalist lines. The result evokes an overwhelming sense of tranquillity and well-being.

This fusion of East and West is also evident in the extensive menu of treatments. Drawn from both Eastern and Western health and beauty traditions, the spa prides itself on using a blend of fresh and organic ingredients for the body and face. The finest massage and essential oils originating from the Far East are selected and used for authentic and relaxing body elixirs and bathing rituals. For instance, the spa's signature Sundari Facial uses active botanical ingredients based on the ayurvedic doshas, which help to determine individual skin needs.

The sumptuous Chedi Massage is one of the spa's signature body treatments. The 60-minute experience entails five different massage styles including shiatsu, Thai, Swedish, Balinese and Hawaiian lomi-lomi. All this is delivered with two highly skilled therapists who work in complete synchrony, and this sublime experience will lull any tired soul into a blissful state of relaxation.

The Balinese Massage is another stellar treatment on the menu. Whether 60- or 90-minutes long, the traditional massage treatment uses stretching as well as palm and thumb pressure techniques. The combination is guaranteed to relieve tension, improve blood flow, ease stress and calm the mind, leaving the body feeling completey energized and renewed.

For those looking to experience a total body ritual, consider the Seaweed Bath. A 30-minute soak in this bath, which is filled with nutrient-rich seaweed and an 'Ocean' blend of bath oil, will leave the skin and body completely nourished and purified.

To ensure that each guest receives a complete and balanced spa experience, every one of the seven treatment rooms features all the spa essentials and includes individual shower and changing facilities. Also, four of these treatment rooms are exclusive spa suites which are nestled within the secluded sanctuary of the resort. An added touch of luxury, these special spa suites come complete with their own private sunken terrazzo baths.

With water gardens and swaying fronds of date palms and the natural dune landscape bordering a private sandy beach, The Spa at The Chedi is a natural retreat for any discerning traveller.

THIS PAGE (FROM TOP): At Chedi Muscat, guests have the option of either relaxing in the luxurious pool or taking a dip in the ocean; the sophisticated style of the spa's treatment rooms ensures a soothing experience.
OPPOSITE (CLOCKWISE FROM TOP): The terrazzo baths in one of the spa's treatment rooms; Arabian décor mixes with chic modern style in the hotel entrance; the stunning water garden where guests can relax and soak in the atmosphere.

Spa Statistics

TYPE OF SPA
Hotel Spa

SPA AREA
824 sq m (8,870 sq ft)

FACILITIES
4 spa suites, 3 single treatment rooms; 1 gymnasium; 2 swimming pools; 2 tennis courts

SIGNATURE TREATMENTS
Chedi Massage, Ocean Ritual, Spirit of Bali

OTHER TREATMENTS AND THERAPIES
Aromatherapy, ayurveda, baths, body scrubs, body wraps, eye treatments, facial treatments, hair treatments, hand and foot treatments, manicures/pedicures, massages, thalassotherapy

SERVICES
Airport transfer, babysitting

LANGUAGES SPOKEN BY THERAPISTS
English

ADMISSION
Membership not required

CONTACT
The Chedi, Muscat
P.O Box 964, Post Code 133
Muscat
Sultanate of Oman
T +968 24 52 44 00
F +968 24 49 34 85
E spa@chedimuscat.com
W www.ghmotels.com

CHI Spa at Shangri-La's Barr Al Jissah Resort & Spa

MUSCAT, SULTANATE OF OMAN

A taste of the mystical Shangri-La can be savoured right in the heart of Oman. Shangri-La's Barr Al Jissah Resort & Spa is an exclusive resort oasis of no less than three five-star hotels, an Omani Heritage Village with activities and exhibits proudly reflecting the local culture, and a 1,000-seat amphitheatre for entertainment under the Arabian sky. Those looking for pampering can indulge at the Shangri-La's own brand of spa—CHI Spa—which constitutes an integral part of the resort experience.

Chi is the ancient Chinese understanding of the universal life force that governs well-being and personal vitality. To maintain good health, it is believed that chi must flow freely within the body; if blocked, illness will follow. The CHI Spa Village draws from the Chinese wellness philosophy of the five elements of earth, fire, water, metal and wood—the balance of these elements is essential for good health. Using Himalayan therapies, the CHI Spa aims for wellness of body, mind and spirit.

Luxury knows no boundaries here too. The Spa features some of the largest and most luxurious private spa suites and villas in Oman. There are 12 treatment villas, each with their own private bathroom, relaxation area and an outdoor garden court complete with loungers and outdoor shower. The villas are totally private—a spa within a spa—with separate entrances, they serve as a personal space and encourage guests to take their time.

Within these rooms of stunning Omani architecture, where the décor is based on Himalayan art and accessories, the signature treatments are equally exotic. Inspired by the healing rituals of the Hor region of Tibet, the Himalayan Healing Stone Massage is a customized ancient massage technique which uses a combination of hot stones—heated in oils and herbs to ground the body and restore vitality—and cool stones, to balance stress. Another treatment from the same tradition is the Mountain Tsampa Rub. This encompasses a barley

scrub where the grain gently removes dead skin cells. Couples are in for a treat with the Yin Yang Couples Massage. This luxurious treatment works to harmonize and pleasantly balance the flow of chi between two people. Experienced in the same room, two therapists coordinate deep rhythmical strokes over each body in perfect synchrony. Focus is given to specific meridians, in order to release tension and restore peace and harmony.

Other treatments available on CHI Spa's menu focus on therapeutic body massage, body toning and detoxification programmes, and speciality skincare treatments. Whatever the choice, each guest undoubtedly leaves relaxed, re-balanced and ready to take on the myriad of activities that the Shangri-La's Barr Al Jissah Resort & Spa has to offer.

THIS PAGE (FROM TOP): The dramatic backdrop is perfect for the grand nature of the resort; inside, the suites feature Arabian style mixed with total comfort.
OPPOSITE (FROM LEFT): CHI Spa's luxurious treatment rooms are decorated with Himalayan-inspired style, the result is a truly relaxing space; the Himalayan healing stone therapy is a signature treatment at CHI.

Spa Statistics

TYPE OF SPA
Resort Spa

SPA AREA
695 sq m (7,480 sq ft)

FACILITIES
4 single indoor treatment villas, 8 double indoor treatment villas; 1 consultation room; 14 relaxation rooms; 1 rasul, 14 Jacuzzis, 1 whirlpool; 4 saunas, 2 steam rooms, 1 hammam; hair salon, nail salon; 2 gymnasiums (one overlooking the beach, another exclusively for Al Husn hotel guests); cardio and aerobic studio, pilates studio; 6 outdoor swimming pools, including children's pools, ice fountains; 4 tennis courts; 1 spa boutique

SIGNATURE TREATMENTS
CHI Balance, Himalayan Healing Stone Massage, Aroma Vitality, Yin Yang Couple's Massage, Mountain Tsampa Rub

OTHER TREATMENTS AND THERAPIES
Body scrubs, body wraps, Chinese therapies, facial treatments, firming and slimming treatments, hair treatments, hand and foot treatments, hot stones therapies, Indonesian therapies, jet-lag treatments, manicures/pedicures, massages, purifying back treatments, reflexology, salon services, scalp treatments

ACTIVITIES AND PROGRAMMES
Aerobics, aquaerobics, cooking classes, scuba diving, snorkelling, tennis classes

SERVICES
Babysitting, childcare, corporate programmes, day-use rooms, gift certificates, personal butler service

SPA CUISINE
A healthy, low fat menu with nutritional information. Chi cuisine incorporates high-energy ingredients that are high in antioxidants.

LANGUAGES SPOKEN BY THERAPISTS
English, Arabic

ADMISSION
Membership available but not required

CONTACT
Shangri-La's Barr Al Jissah Resort & Spa
PO Box 644, PC 113
Muscat
Sultanate of Oman
T +968 24 77 66 66
F +968 24 77 66 77
E slmu@shangri-la.com
W www.shangri-la.com/spa

Four Seasons Hotel Doha

DOHA, QATAR

Stepping away from the turquoise waters of the Arabian Gulf, through the resort's expansive archways and Romanesque columns, you are led directly into the Zen-inspired minimalist interiors of The Spa and Wellness Centre at Four Seasons Hotel Doha. It's easy to find as the refreshing scent of bergamot essential oil and the sounds of cascading water walls act as a sensual guide.

Here, an ambience of well-being encompasses the space; the décor is themed around the five elements of water, fire, earth, metal and wood. This theme is reflected throughout the three-storey Spa and Wellness Centre, not only in the spa's design, but also in the treatments and cuisine on offer.

The menu of treatments could leave even the most experienced spa-goer lost for choice. A good choice is the Radiance Ritual named Beaming Happiness, or the Wholeness Ritual—Balance and Harmony. The 150-minute Purity Ritual, Being Free, is a full-body massage beginning with the back, that works deep into the muscles, helping to remove accumulated toxins and waste. A fabulous facial follows, using the cleansing properties of Argiletz clay and balancing plant essences to purify the skin.

The Five Elements in Harmony with the Seasons is the Spa's signature treatment. As its name implies, guests can experience the four seasons in this single treatment. First, winter comes in a cooling and invigorating exfoliation for the body, hands and feet. Spring brings forth a nourishing

THIS PAGE (FROM LEFT): The sumptuous spa reception creates the perfect welcome to spa guests; inside the spa, the style reflects the five basic elements. This stylish fountain represents the element of water.
OPPOSITE (FROM TOP): Four Seasons Hotel Doha is an example of stylish and opulent Arabian design; the hydrotherapy pool offers a soothing underwater massage.

bath while summer warms the body with a hot stone massage, followed by a relaxing wrap rich in minerals and algae, leaving the skin looking and feeling toned for autumn.

The 60-minute signature Earth Body Massage is a mark well above the rest. It combines the healing power of touch with unique techniques of slow, smooth strokes. The massage works in harmony with natural plant oils and essences to encourage an increase in lymphatic circulation and to clear blockages in the energy channels of the body. Emotional and physical tension are relieved, and the mind, body and spirit are balanced.

The Spa and Wellness Centre also boasts the first hydrotherapy lounge in Qatar—the region's most extensive hydrotherapy hideaway, surrounded by floor-to-ceiling windows and glass doors that lead out to the hotel's private beach. The lounge includes cool and warm plunge pools, a Kneipp foot bath, heated laconium beds, a laconium room, a colour therapy room and a meditation room. There is also the hydrotherapy pool where warm air jets pummel at the body to effectively release tension, ease muscle and joint pain and improve circulation. Along with everything else the innovative hydrotherapy lounge has to offer, spa guests can be confident that this spa experience will be second to none.

Spa Statistics

TYPE OF SPA
Hotel Spa

SPA AREA
3,160 sq m (34,000 sq ft)

FACILITIES
5 single indoor treatment rooms, 2 double indoor treatment rooms, 2 spa suites, 1 Thai massage room; 1 meditation room; 2 relaxation areas (1 for women, 1 for men); 1 colour therapy room; 1 cold plunge pool, 1 warm plunge pool, 1 hydrotherapy pool, 1 Kneipp foot bath; 1 sauna, 1 steam room, 1 tepidarium for body scrubs and wraps, 1 laconium; gymnasium; 1 aerobics studio; 1 outdoor swimming pool with whirlpools, hot tubs and adjacent children's pool; 2 outdoor tennis courts, 2 squash courts, beauty salon

SIGNATURE TREATMENTS
Earth Body Massage, Five Elements in Harmony with the Seasons,

OTHER TREATMENTS AND THERAPIES
Aromatherapy, baths, body scrubs, body wraps, eye treatments, facial treatments, hand and foot treatments, hot stone therapies, hydrotherapy, Indonesian therapies, lymphatic drainage massage, massages, reflexology, Thai therapies, thalassotherapy, waxing

ACTIVITIES AND PROGRAMMES
Golf, pilates, squash, tennis, yoga

SERVICES
Childcare

SPA CUISINE
Après Spa Café offers herbal tea or coffee, energy drinks, healthy juices and light meals.

LANGUAGES SPOKEN BY THERAPISTS
English, Arabic

ADMISSION
Membership available but not required

CONTACT
Four Seasons Resort Doha
The Corniche
P.O. Box 24665
Doha
Qatar
T +974 494 8888
F +974 494 8282
E spa.doh@fourseasons.com
W www.fourseasons.com

Mövenpick Ulysse Palace & Thalasso

DJERBA, TUNISIA

Perched on the edge of Tunisia is the small idyllic island of Djerba. Here, offering the perfect spa escape is the magnificent Mövenpick Ulysse Palace & Thalasso. There is no better location than this island paradise—so described by Homer as 'the island of the blissfully happy'—for a haven of complete relaxation and well-being. Floating in the cerulean Mediterranean Sea, laced with beautiful sandy beaches—just 5 kilometres (3 miles) from the coast of Tunisia—the jewel in this Mövenpick resort's crown is the newly renovated Thalasso Spa that provides truly innovative and modern water-based spa therapy.

From the outside, the ochre of the resort walls lies strikingly against the clear blue and never-ending Mediterranean sky. The minimal style boasts lean, simple lines and curves that echo the traditional Tunisian architecture. Together they take the eye on a pleasing journey, easing the mind into a state of complete calmness. Palm trees grow majestically all around this 5-star resort hotel and enhance the Arabian ambience. Strategically located on the edge of a long beach, just metres away from the sea, the paradisical island setting offers an extensive range of sunbathing and leisure options. Given these gorgeous surrounds, it may be tempting to just lie back in a poolside deckchair, soak in the year-round sun and watch the distant coconut trees sway in the sea breeze. But the Thalasso Spa beckons, for within its stylish walls even more indulgences of the senses await.

One of the few genuine thalassotherapy centres outside of France, this spa in Tunisia calls upon the healing nature of the surrounding ocean—as any genuine thalassotherapy centre should—to heal and pamper its guests. Whether it is to soothe rheumatic pain, for general weight loss or simply to de-stress and improve overall well-being, the Thalasso provides a host of facilities and sea-based therapies that use seawater, seaweed and algae. All treatments are administered by professional and experienced therapists, and qualified doctors are on hand to give medical advice and consultation. The 3,500-square-metre (37,673-square-foot) centre

consists of no less than three indoor pools and extensive water-based treatment facilities.

In the traditional Turkish hammam, guests are able to relax in the soothing heat and enjoy the surrounding sea view. Composed of three rooms, the temperatures vary between 30°C–50°C (86°F–122°F). The heat works its natural magic by warming up the body to remove toxins, and to soften dead skin cells. Once the body has adjusted to the heat, the hammam scrub ensues. In this final stage, therapists use the traditional kehsa glove to scrub and cleanse the body, leaving the skin soft and supple. After, there is little to do other than rest and re-balance in the hammam area before a refreshing cup of mint tea concludes this age-old practice. Next door, the two saunas of varying dry heat offer an alternative Arabian spa experience.

The multifarious healing elements of the sea are also used in the range of body wraps that appear on the spa menu. Treatments vary from partial- or full-body algae wraps and in each, the body is completely enveloped in hot algae from the world-renowned Phytomer spa product range. The powerful nutrients of algae are known to help guard the skin from impurities and eliminate toxins. The warm body wrap itself can also be used to ease pains brought about by osteoarthritis and rheumatism.

There are a total of 12 treatment rooms at the Thalasso and, no matter how short the visit, the Mandara Massage is a highly recommended treatment. This treat for the whole body combines shiatsu with other traditional massage techniques from around the world. Using ancestral methods and essential oils chosen specifically for relaxation, two therapists simultaneously massage the body using not only their hands but their arms, elbows and fingers as well. By kneading, stretching and applying various pressure techniques over the body, the massage effectively leaves the mind, body and spirit completely revitalized.

THIS PAGE (FROM TOP): Sunset creates a beautiful ambience at the resort; part of the extensive list of facilities at the spa, the hammam encompasses a hot and cold room where guests can relax as the alternating temperature works its magic.
OPPOSITE: The indoor pool, a celebration of Tunisian style, offers an escape from the sun.

In between treatments, or to end a day of pampering, visit the La Tisanerie Thalasso Bar. Here guests can sip a refreshing cup of tea or the famous Mövenpick coffee, savour the sea view and enjoy the moment of unhurried peace. Elsewhere in the 264-room resort, guests can sample international and local cuisines in one of the three restaurants. For international cuisine the Ulysse Restaurant caters for breakfast and dinner. The Tunisian restaurant, El Malouf, offers local specialities in stylish surrounds and Neptune Restaurant provides the freshest seafood from the surrounding sea. For the more actively-inclined, activities include yoga classes, beach volleyball, surfing and horse riding. All this can be arranged by the helpful and friendly resort staff and enjoyed at the resort before venturing off to explore the rest of the island of Djerba.

The island itself makes for a superb holiday destination and is situated in the southeast of Tunisia on the Gulf of Gabes in the Mediterranean Sea. Growing in international popularity, the destination is loved for its eternal sunshine and unending sandy beaches that cover a huge area of 514 square kilometres (198 square miles). The capital, Houmt Souk, is just 10 kilometres (6 miles) away from the Mövenpick resort. It makes for a perfect day-trip, with its numerous bars and restaurants, and authentic souks (bazaars) that will whet any traveller's appetite.

For those in search of a more cultural experience, the arid, sun-baked region of Matmata is nearby. A historic place named after a Berber tribe, the site features troglodyte 'homes' that sit 5–10 metres (16–33 feet) beneath its lunar landscape. Carved out of rock, Matmata is a must for *Star Wars* fans as this is where the movie was made.

Even closer to the resort, a round of golf is another perfect way to spend the day. The Djerba Golf Club is just an 8-minute drive from the hotel. It offers three challenging courses of a manageable nine holes each. With a fantastic view of the sea, acacias, and palm trees, it is a great way to relax and take in the delightful island of Djerba.

After the sun has set, try your luck at the big casino of Djerba just three minutes away from the hotel. It has a gaming room of 18 tables, 160 slot machines, a restaurant and a bar. Those looking for authentic Moorish coffee could get a cup here.

Whatever is decided upon, the unique destination, the authentic Thalasso Spa and the therapies it offers will ensure a memorable experience not easily forgotten.

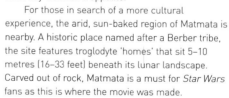

THIS PAGE: The hydropool where guests can enjoy an underwater massage and other benefits from the spa's thalassotherapy range of treatments.
OPPOSITE (CLOCKWISE FROM TOP): The resort sits comfortably in its natural surroundings of the beautiful island of Djerba; the Mandara Massage features techniques drawn from all around the world including shiatsu; a luxury suite at the resort is fully equipped to provide a memorable stay at Djerba.

Spa Statistics

TYPE OF SPA
Resort Spa

SPA AREA
3,500 sq m (37,670 sq ft)

FACILITIES:
12 treatment rooms; 2 consultation rooms; 1 relaxation room; 10 hydro-massage baths, 4 affusion showers; 2 saunas, 1 hammam; 1 seawater swimming pool, 1 pool with hydro-massage jets, gymnasium, 1 spa boutique

SIGNATURE TREATMENTS
Phytomer Algae Body Wrap, Mandara Massage

OTHER TREATMENTS AND THERAPIES
Body wraps, body scrubs, facial treatments, hand and foot treatments, hydrotherapy, massages, thalassotherapy

ACTIVITIES
Aquaerobics, beach volleyball, canoeing, golf, horse riding, petanque, surfing, water sports, yoga

SERVICES
Babysitting, childcare

LANGUAGES SPOKEN BY THERAPISTS
English

ADMISSION
Exclusively for resort guests

CONTACT
Mövenpick Ulysse Palace & Thalasso
Route Touristique
Plage de Sidi Mehrez, BP 239
4128 Djerba
Tunisia
T +216 75 758 777
F +216 75 757 850
E resort.djerba@moevenpick.com
W www.moevenpick-hotels.com

Jamilah Spa & Leisure Centre at Al Maha Desert Resort & Spa

DUBAI, UNITED ARAB EMIRATES

Since time immemorial, nomadic Bedouin tribes have traversed the rolling sand dunes of the Arabian Desert. Living off camel's milk and succulent dates from palm trees in oases, they made their home in elaborate encampments they set up along their way. In keeping with their indigenous lifestyle, Al Maha Desert Resort & Spa established a cluster of luxurious Bedouin-style accommodation offering total privacy and facilities that evoke the spirit of these wanderers of the vast Arabian Desert.

Located in a 225-square-kilometre (87-square mile) desert conservation reserve, some 45 minutes from Dubai, the Al Maha resort is an oasis unto itself. Set amongst lush indigenous vegetation, tranquil water features and warming tones of the sand, this thoughtfully designed resort melds seamlessly into the undulating dunes that surround it. Guests can enjoy uninterrupted views of the desert and the mountains in the distance whilst luxuriating in the unique Arabian setting.

The latest addition to this award-winning resort is the Jamilah Spa & Leisure Centre. Nestled in the dunes near the resort's main building, the spa offers private treatment rooms discreetly linked to public areas by soft timber decks. A rim-flow relaxation pool beckons in between treatments; an interior Jacuzzi, a plunge pool, a sauna and steam room overlook the landscaped gardens; and shared with the resort is the expansive main pool. To conserve the desert's most precious commodity, all water at Al Maha is fully recycled and returned to its groundwater source via an innovative irrigation system. Al Maha's efforts to protect the environment has earned it numerous conservation accolades

from the travel industry; the resort won a World Legacy Award in 2004, and is reputed to be one of the finest eco-tourism resorts in the Middle East.

Desert plants and minerals nourished the Bedouin for centuries. Jamilah Spa tapped into this ancient wisdom to formulate its own range of spa products, called "Timeless", which it uses in all its treatments. "Timeless" products comprise pure Arabian frankincense—a distillate of the sap of the boswellia tree—and sweet oil from the ubiquitous date. For the Bedouin, the date was a cure-all from the gods. It was used as an antiseptic for wounds, a poultice for burns and a muscle relaxant for expectant mothers, in addition to being a source of food on long, dry journeys through the desert. Today, guests at Jamilah Spa benefit from the curative and restorative properties of this miracle fruit and soothing frankincense in the "Timeless" products which were developed in the research facilities of world spa leaders Babor in Aachen, Germany.

There is no better way to revel in the delights of "Timeless" spa products than sampling one of Jamilah's signature treatments. At the top of the list is the "Timeless" Traditions Four Hands Body Treatment. Two therapists simultaneously knead the body from head to toe using a melting combination of Swedish and deep tissue massage techniques.

Guests are primed for this experience with cooling foot and face packs filled with fresh dates as well as a light application of face cream and golden eye gel. After the 90-minute body massage, a calming facial massage and cooling pre-sun face treatment prepares you for the desert's unrelenting rays.

Another of Jamilah's most popular treatments is the Desert Sand Herb Rasul Treatment. Executed in a purpose-built rasul room, this treatment involves coating your body in mineral-rich clay concocted from the "Timeless" range of products. Once you are swathed in clay, a gentle cloud of aromatic steam is emitted into the rasul room where you lie for just

THIS PAGE (CLOCKWISE FROM TOP): The double treatment room provides ultimate privacy while allowing couples to share the experience; guests staying in the Emirates Suite are attended to by their own private staff and can enjoy total seclusion and spectacular views across the desert; a calming treatment in the meditative silence of the spa's own rasul room.
OPPOSITE: Jamilah Spa's main pool area blends perfectly with its desert surroundings and appears as though an oasis.

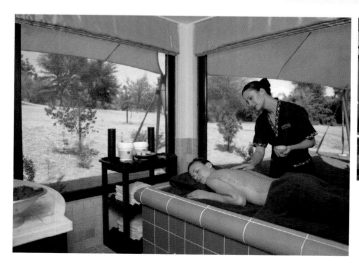

THIS PAGE (CLOCKWISE FROM LEFT): Enjoy a massage from the extensive spa list and take in the desert's breathtaking beauty at the same time; the Jacuzzi provides the ideal place to unwind before your treatment begins; palm trees around Al Maha's suites ensure privacy as well as providing essential shade from the sun. OPPOSITE: After your treatment allow your body to re-balance in the relaxation lounge before slowly returning to reality.

under an hour, absorbing all the natural goodness of the clay. While your skin re-balances, mood-sensitive lighting in maroon, pink, green, blue and lilac calm the senses, and a meditative silence pervades the room. When the treatment is over, a delicate massage rubs off the clay and exfoliates the skin at the same time, while a specially prepared body moisturizer leaves you feeling fresh and supple.

For optimal results, it is recommended that you do both rasul and "Timeless" treatments, in that order. Rasul removes dead cells from the skin's surface while "Timeless" strengthens and tightens the tissue. Together, these treatments are most effective in keeping your skin firm, smooth and soft.

Other treatments at Jamilah include Desert Pre- and After-Sun Care. Proper sun care ensures that you glow from the kiss of the Arabian sun without succumbing to its harshness. With the Pre-Sun Care treatment, the body is exfoliated and covered in sunscreen. In After-Sun Care, a body mask and balm soothes your skin. As the body re-balances, guests enjoy a reflexology massage.

Jamilah's massage menu is extensive. You can choose from a De-stress Back Massage, a Manual Lymphatic Drainage, a Desert Aroma Massage, a Mothers-To-Be Massage as well as the traditional all-time favourite, Swedish Massage. A perfect accompaniment to any massage is a facial. Jamilah offers its very own Al Maha "Timeless" Frankincense Aroma Facial, which involves a clarifying mask and a thorough scalp, face and neck massage. Alternatively, you can try the Refreshing Aroma Facial, a 60-minute aromatherapy lymphatic massage. This facial is especially good for skin which has been exposed to damaging elements such as the sun or air-conditioning. Babor's exquisite "Timeless" products are used in each of Jamilah's treatments.

Allow yourself at least half a day at the spa, giving you an hour to enjoy the surroundings before your treatments begin. To prepare for your treatment, spa staff suggest that you first relax in the hot whirlpool or unwind in the sauna or steam room, and then splash yourself with an invigorating cold shower or a dip in the icy plunge pool. Drinking copious amounts of water or fresh juices is also a good idea, especially before aroma-hydrotherapy treatments. The more relaxed and hydrated you are before a treatment, the more you will benefit from it. After your treatment, you can rest in the relaxation area and allow the full effect of your treatment to sink in and slowly slide back into reality.

Al Maha gets its name from the Arabian oryx, the spear-horned desert antelope which proliferates in the presence of life-giving water. This regal animal is regularly sighted in the dunes around the resort, a testament to the rejuvenating forces which emanate from this delightful place.

Spa Statistics

TYPE OF SPA
Resort Spa

SPA AREA
824 sq m (8,870 sq ft)

FACILITIES
2 double treatment rooms; 2 single treatment rooms,
1 hydrotheraphy room, 1 rasul treatment room,
1 outdoor swimming pool, 1 indoor Jacuzzi, 1 sauna,
1 steam room, 1 plunge pool, 1 gymnasium, 1 manicure
and pedicure area, 1 relaxation lounge, 1 fruit bar

SIGNATURE TREATMENTS
Timeless Traditions Four Hands Body Treatment,
Desert Sand Herb Rasul Treatment

OTHER TREATMENTS AND THERAPIES
Desert Pre-Sun Care, Desert After-Sun Care, De-
stress Back Massage, Manual Lymphatic Drainage,
Mother-To-Be Massage, Desert Aroma Massage,
Swedish Massage, Reflexology, Al Maha Frankincense
Aroma Facial, Refreshing Aroma Facial, Salt Body
Peeling, Desert Tonic, Aroma Hydrotherapy, Spa
Pedicure and Manicure

SPA CUISINE
Spa menu comprises a healthy selection of food and
beverages. Special dietary requirements can be
catered to on request.

ACTIVITIES AND PROGRAMMES
Camel rides, wildlife drives, dune drives, archery,
falconry, horse rides, personal fitness programmes

SERVICES
Private dining and functions in sand dunes, corporate
programmes

LANGUAGES SPOKEN BY THERAPISTS
English, German, Japanese, Thai, Tagalog, Mandarin,
Afrikaans, Bahasa Melayu

ADMISSION
Exclusively for resort guests

CONTACT
Al Maha Desert Resort & Spa
PO Box 7631
Dubai
United Arab Emirates
T +971 4 303 4222
F +971 4 343 9696
E almaha@emirates.com
W www.al-maha.com

Assawan Spa at Burj Al Arab

DUBAI, UNITED ARAB EMIRATES

Arising out of the waters on its own man-made island, the sail soars 321 metres (1,050 feet) high. Dominating the impressive Dubai coastal skyline, Burj Al Arab has become an icon of luxury and prosperity. Built in the shape of an Arabian dhow sail, this five-star deluxe hotel, located some 280 metres (920 feet) offshore, is the ultimate refuge.

Acknowledged as the world's most luxurious hotel, as well as the world's tallest hotel building, it was built with groundbreaking technology. Architects rose to the enormous challenge and created the iconic sail façade using Teflon-coated fibreglass, the first time such material has been used vertically and to such an extent. Burj Al Arab is not only visually spectacular from the outside, its interior is equally, if not more breathtaking. Only the finest materials, the most intricate craftsmanship and attention to detail can be found within.

This high standard extends to the service. There is a chauffeur-driven Rolls Royce, a discreet in-suite check-in service, a private reception desk on every floor and a staff of highly-trained and multilingual butlers available; guests are guaranteed an impeccable, round-the-clock service. All these things contribute to an unforgettable experience.

This excellent personalized service can be found at the hotel's Assawan Spa. Ascending the sail, the lift arrives on the 18th floor, and opens its doors to sheer opulence and decadent comfort. The Assawan Spa at Burj Al Arab is a haven for those seeking weight loss, stress reduction or simply a place to relax and enjoy spa therapy.

The reception alone is awesome. Guests are welcomed by the magnificent mosaic domed ceiling, the ornately tiled corridors and a stunning and spacious lounge. Exotic scents draw you deeper into the sanctuary and the sense of relaxation pervades the air. The extravagant décor is reminiscent of bathing pools used by ancient Middle Eastern civilizations. To unwind, spa guests can enjoy a soak in the bubbling pools, which are surrounded by vast regal columns that hold the high ceiling, whilst overlooking the spectacular view. The Assawan Spa is as breathtaking as the rest of the hotel.

Through the ages, assawan granite has been used for its magical properties. Healers have used it to cure, soothe and invigorate those in search of radiance and vitality. Deriving its name from this miraculous stone, the Assawan Spa promises an experience that will stimulate the senses, rejuvenate the body and refresh the mind.

From within the 14 treatment rooms, each guest's well-being is of primary concern. At the outset, individual needs are discussed, and all treatments are tailored to suit the guest. Plus, the products used at the Assawan Spa are from the E'SPA and La Prairie ranges, which are synonymous with high quality and outstanding results.

Assawan Spa's professional therapists are highly trained to carry out all treatments from the extensive spa menu. There is a variety of facial treatments, manicures and pedicures, as well as full-body massages, scrubs, wraps and rituals that are drawn from many cultures across the globe. Take, for example, the Muscle Relaxer. This is an ayurvedic treatment that uses the inimitable healing properties of herbs and plants. The session lasts for 60 minutes and begins with a sea salt and aromatherapy oil exfoliation, this is then followed by a nourishing body mask made from an infusion of plants and spices. This recipe warms and hydrates the skin and helps to relieve aching muscles and joints, leaving the body feeling nimble and refreshed.

There is a treatment for every inch of your body at Assawan Spa, even for the hips and thighs. Befittingly called the Concentrated Hip & Thigh Treatment, this is a 60-minute, ladies-only massage that works on the circulatory and lymphatic systems using E'SPA products. It focuses on the areas of the body that are prone to blockages, which cause cellulite, fluid retention and uneven skin texture.

Nothing is too indulgent at the Assawan Spa. The Caviar Body Treatment, one of the Spa's signature treatments, is a 1-hour-15-minute total extravagance. Guests can lie relaxed and take in the view whilst being completely covered in the mixture,

THIS PAGE (CLOCKWISE FROM TOP): Now an icon of luxury, the dhow sail-shaped hotel dominates the Dubai coastal skyline; Arabian details decorate the Jacuzzi and wet area where guests can unwind before treatment; Assawan Spa's Diwania library, proving that the spa is a truly holistic escape.
OPPOSITE: Regal columns hold the high ceiling while guests unwind in the bathing pool and take in the impressive view.

content in the knowledge that caviar actually has an immediate and long-term firming action.

The Assawan Spa certainly has something for everyone. For busy executives who have some free time on their hands, there is a specially tailored package—the Reviver Ritual. This 2-hour-15-minute treatment promises to leave any tired businessman or woman feeling energized, invigorated and harmonized. The package consists of an E'SPA aromatherapy massage, a pressure point foot massage and a mini facial treatment.

Expectant mothers can also find suitable treatments. New Beginnings is a long and relaxing 2-hour-30-minute treatment for pregnant mothers who are in need of a little pampering. Designed especially for pregnancy, it includes a pre-natal treatment and a pedicure for those tired feet. Thoughtfully, the Pre-Natal Treatment avoids the use of essential oils. This is advised by the Aromatherapy Organization Council. Instead, the treatment uses a

combination of a calming and healing calendula infused oil, various muds and creams as well as advanced massage techniques over the safe areas of the body. The resulting total body treatment completely relaxes the mother-to-be and tones her skin, creating an overall state of well-being.

Those looking for more active ways to relax may consider the extensive programmes and activities offered at the Assawan Health Club. The very latest equipment fills the vast gymnasiums, while fitness professionals lead every kind of exercise class, from aerobics through to yoga. In fact, the Health Club can also put together a personalized exercise programme for each guest.

After a relaxing massage or a great workout, retire to the Amphitheatre lounge—so named because it resembles a Roman Amphitheatre with its ornamental columns and marble backdrop—with a glass of refreshing fruit cocktail or a light snack. Those keen on reading can choose a good book from the Diwania Library, which offers an extensive selection of Arabic and a wide range of European books. There is even a custom-made snooker table for those who fancy a game.

Outside, beautiful white beaches await those who like to feel the sand between their toes. A private beach as well as an outdoor pool are for your exclusive use. Water sports are available at the Jumeirah Beach Hotel which is just a short walk or buggy-ride away. Guests can try anything from wind surfing to kayaking to deep-sea fishing. Alternatively, there is a yacht at your disposal.

Whatever you decide to do, you will, without a doubt, walk out of the Assawan Spa feeling absolutely relaxed, pampered and rejuvenated.

Spa Statistics

TYPE OF SPA
Hotel Spa

SPA AREA
6,805 sq m (73,250 sq ft)

FACILITIES
14 indoor treatment rooms; 1 relaxation area;
2 hydrobath rooms, 2 plunge pools, 2 whirlpools;
2 saunas, 2 steam rooms; 2 solariums; Frank Provost
Hair Salon, 2 manicure/pedicure rooms; 1 exercise
studio, 1 fully equipped gymnasium; 2 indoor relaxation
swimming pools, 1 outdoor swimming pool; 2 spa
boutiques (1 for hotel merchandise, 1 with skincare
products, candles and perfumes)

SIGNATURE TREATMENTS
La Prairie Eye Bliss Treatment

OTHER TREATMENTS AND THERAPIES
Anti-cellulite treatments, aromatherapy, ayurveda,
back treatments, body scrubs, body wraps, facial
treatments, hand and foot treatments, holistic
treatments, hot stone therapies, lymphatic drainage
massages, manicures/pedicures, massages, pre-natal
treatments, reflexology

SPA CUISINE
Non-alcoholic beverages, light snacks

ACTIVITIES AND PROGRAMMES
Aerobics, aqua classes, yoga

SERVICES
Internet access, library, personalized exercise
programme

LANGUAGES SPOKEN BY THERAPISTS
English, Afrikaans, Arabic, Balinese, French, Bahasa
Indonesian, Tagalog

ADMISSION
Open to guests and members only, outside guests
for Rituals only

CONTACT
Assawan Spa at Burj Al Arab
P.O. Box 74147
Dubai
United Arab Emirates
T +971 4 301 7338
F +971 4 301 7318
E BAAassawan@jumeirah.com
W www.jumeirah.com

Cleopatra's Spa

DUBAI, UNITED ARAB EMIRATES

Situated in the luxurious Egyptian-style complex of Wafi City, in the heart of Dubai, Cleopatra's Spa offers a purely indulgent experience. It is the largest day spa in the United Arab Emirates and can ably accommodate every individual's needs with its vast array of Arabian as well as international treatments.

Guests can capture a truly authentic Arabian experience in the spa's own luxurious rasul chamber. This innovative and sumptuous treatment blends ancient Middle Eastern tradition with beauty and relaxation. The body is first completely covered with a special mud mixture made from medicinal earth. Whilst seated in cool ceramic chairs, guests then relax in a dome-shaped heated chamber, under a star-studded ceiling, while a warm and comforting herbal steam gently opens and cleanses the pores. A shower simulating tropical rain washes away the mud leaving the body feeling totally renewed.

The spa's inspiration is Ancient Egypt and the Queen herself, but there are treatments drawn from the world over. For instance, the spa's signature Javanese Royal Treatment. This 90-minute ritual originated from Bali and was designed for brides to soften and lighten their skin. The treatment begins with a traditional Balinese Massage with tropical oils to energize the body. A fruit and herbal mixture is then applied to exfoliate and smoothen the skin. Fresh yoghurt is then applied in order to moisturize and nourish the body and to remove the herbal mixture. Finally, a frangipani lotion is massaged gently into the skin. For a regal-style pampering there is the option of extending this treatment with a 20-minute soak in the bronze Cleopatra Bath.

Baths are one of the more innovative and luxurious treatments you can enjoy at Cleopatra's Spa. For an average of 30 minutes, you can relax in a

jet bath infused with selected aromatic oils and herbs. The Stress-Away Ocean Bath will soothe and revive the body and the mind with a blend of fragrances such as melissa, bergamot and camomile. For those wanting to de-tox, the Detox Ocean Bath has been devised especially to combat the common problem of water retention. It will leave the body refreshed and even a little slimmer.

Beside these treatments, there are advanced anti-ageing facials, well-being massages as well as various slimming treatments to choose from. The spa uses only the best and most luxurious products including the Elemis, O'lys Light Therapy and Ionithermie product ranges.

Cleopatra's Spa offers complete privacy with separate spas for both men and women, seven days a week. Housed in the Pyramids at Wafi City, guests can also visit the elite hair salon, Hair@Pyramids, or join the fully-equipped gym at Pharoah's Club.

THIS PAGE (CLOCKWISE FROM TOP): Capture a true Arabian experience and enjoy a soak in the luxurious Cleopatra Bath; Cleopatra's Spa provides a wide range of massages drawn from all over the world; natural ingredients are used to nourish the skin and enhance the overall feeling of well-being.
OPPOSITE (FROM TOP): Guests can drift off in the ambience of the treatment room while in the capable hands of the spa's experienced staff; alternate between sauna and plunge pool or relax in the Jacuzzi before your treatment.

Spa Statistics

TYPE OF SPA
Day Spa

SPA AREA
Female spa 850 sq m (9,150 sq ft)
Male spa 400 sq m (4,300 sq ft)

FACILITIES
Female spa: 14 treatment rooms, 2 dry flotation rooms, 1 Thai massage room, 1 Ayurvedic treatment room; relaxation area, 1 relaxation/waterbed room; 1 hydro bath, 1 Jacuzzi, 1 plunge pool; 1 rasul chamber; 1 tanning room; 1 nail salon
Male spa: 4 treatment rooms, 1 dry floatation room, 1 Thai massage room, 1 Ayurvedic treatment room; relaxation room; 1 hydro bath, 1 Jacuzzi, 1 plunge pool, 1 sauna, 1 steam room; 1 barber salon, 1 nail salon

SIGNATURE TREATMENTS
Royal Javanese Treatment with Bronze Cleopatra Bath

OTHER TREATMENTS AND THERAPIES
Ayurveda, body rituals, body wraps, ear candling, Elemis Advanced Performance facials, Elemis Visible Brilliance Facial, hot stone massage, international massages, Ionithermie, Olys Light Facials, St Tropez Tanning

SPA CUISINE
Spa menu comprises a healthy selection of food and drink

SERVICES
Crèche available by advance request, gift certificates, spa packages

LANGUAGES SPOKEN BY THERAPISTS
English, Arabic, Chinese, Japanese, Tagalog, Thai, Hindi, Romanian, Bahasa Indonesian, Russian

ADMISSION
By reservation only. Entrance to relaxation and wet areas is complimentary with most treatments. Membership is available on a quarterly and annual basis.

CONTACT
Cleopatra's Spa
Pyramid's Health and Leisure
Wafi City
Dubai
United Arab Emirates
T +971 4 324 7700/0000
F +971 4 324 4611
W www.waficity.com

The Grand Spa at the Grand Hyatt

DUBAI, UNITED ARAB EMIRATES

In Dubai, The Grand Spa is where business meets pleasure. Located on the atrium level of the 674-room Grand Hyatt Dubai, it is the leisure and exercise complex of one of the largest, grandest conference and convention centres in the Middle East.

Set in a city conference resort hotel within 15 hectares (37 acres) of landscaped gardens, The Grand Spa is an oasis within an oasis. After a hard day's work—or shopping—The Grand Spa offers the perfect way to unwind and relax. In each of the six Zen-inspired treatment rooms, a team of qualified therapists are on hand to provide an extensive range of facial and body treatments, massages and a unique set of Aromasoul massages.

Spa guests can experience Aromasoul, a unique system of sensorial well-being rituals that combine rare blends of essential oils and natural extracts. A treatment concept available exclusively at The Grand Spa, Aromasoul features in four lavish treatments and are inspired by Indian, Arabian, Oriental and Mediterranean traditions. Inspired by the Arabian healing methods of the ancient tribes of the Sahara,

THIS PAGE (FROM TOP): The Grand Spa offers a vast array of massage treatments, from Swedish and Balinese to deep tissue and sports massages, as well as the unique Aromasoul rituals, every need is catered for; the 20-metre indoor lap pool, complete with an underwater sound system, offers enjoyable exercise. OPPOSITE (FROM TOP): Zen-inspired décor creates a calm sanctuary for the busy executive; the spa's signature treatment, the Hot Stone Massage, promotes a sense of relaxation and heightened well-being; if peckish post-treatment, the hotel provides a huge selection of cuisines with its 14 restaurants and bars.

the 3-hour Aromasoul Arabian Retreat is a profoundly calming and renewing experience. It begins with a full-body Aromasoul massage ritual, which includes an exfoliation, followed by a rhythmic-styled massage to ignite inner vitality, and finishes with a rehydrating and replenishing Action Sublime Facial to enhance the skin's complexion.

The Grand Spa is also renowned for its signature Hot Stone Massage, a deeply soothing therapy which uses heated basalt stones and therapeutic essential oils to detoxify, relax and drain the body of impurities.

Guests can indulge in a half- or full-day retreat and personalized spa programmes can be individually designed. Whether the goal is relaxation, rejuvenation, to reduce stress, or detoxify, the menu will cater for any need. Male guests are cared for with the Gentleman's Retreat, which offers an all-over exfoliation, a massage and facial treatment. In the cooler months, guests can choose to have treatments outdoors amid the hotel's landscaped gardens.

The Grand Spa offers numerous ways to keep fit. You can swim laps, run along the 450-metre track and enjoy the landscaped gardens, or try a game of tennis. Also, the world-class Dubai Creek Golf Course is a mere 5 minutes from the hotel.

Just 10 minutes drive from the international airport and Dubai's World Trade Centre, and just a three-minute walk from the adjacent Wafi Shopping Centre, The Grand Spa at the Grand Hyatt Dubai gives new meaning to mixing business with pleasure.

Spa Statistics

TYPE OF SPA
Hotel Spa

SPA AREA
2,156 sq m (23,210 sq ft) indoor spa area
28,457 sq m (306,310 sq ft) indoor/outdoor area

FACILITIES
6 treatment rooms; 3 relaxation lounges; 3 Jacuzzis, 2 plunge pools; 2 saunas, 2 steam rooms; 24-hour gymnasium, 1 indoor lap pool (with underwater music), 1 outdoor swimming pool, 1 children's outdoor swimming pool with slides, 1 toddler's pool; 4 floodlit tennis courts, 2 indoor squash courts, 1 450-metre running track

SIGNATURE TREATMENTS
Aromasoul Arabian Retreat, Hot Stone Massage, fusion deals

OTHER TREATMENTS AND THERAPIES
Anti-ageing treatments, anti-cellulite treatments, aromasoul massages, body scrubs, body wraps, facial treatments, firming treatments, hand and foot treatments, hot stone therapies, jet-lag treatment, manicures/pedicures, massages, mud therapies, reflexology, specialized treatments such as reiki

ACTIVITIES AND PROGRAMMES
Kickboxing, personal training, pilates, squash lessons, swimming lessons, tennis lessons, yoga

SERVICES
Children's daily activities, The Kidz Club

LANGUAGES SPOKEN BY THERAPISTS
English, Arabic, Afrikaans, French, Hindu, Italian, Romanian, Russian, Tagalog, Thai

ADMISSION
Day passes available

CONTACT
The Grand Spa
Atrium Level
Grand Hyatt Dubai
PO Box 7978
Dubai
United Arab Emirates
T +971 4 317 2333
F +971 4 317 1235
E dubai.grand@hyattintl.com
W www.dubai.grand.hyatt.com

Jebel Ali Golf Resort & Spa

DUBAI, UNITED ARAB EMIRATES

The Jebel Ali Golf Resort & Spa, comprising both the Jebel Ali Hotel and the Palm Tree Court & Spa, is a 394-room resort situated on the golden shores of the Arabian Gulf. The beach stretches 800 metres (2,625 feet) in length and this 'Leading Hotel' is further complemented by landscaped gardens, ponds, and a 9-hole golf course. A stay at a golf resort does not necessarily mean putting on the greens all the time. At the Jebel Ali Golf Resort & Spa, there is the option of a spa retreat at the two-storey purpose-built wellness facility, simply named The Spa.

Set within the Palm Tree Court & Spa and the Jebel Ali Hotel, just a few steps from the beach, this 'Leading Spa' is a stunning and luxurious sanctuary, offering a combination of classic treatments and innovative spa technology. There are over 40 face and body treatments available, each designed to help you relax, rejuvenate and re-energize. A leading UK spa brand, Elemis is used alongside Wild Earth products

and Ionithermie slimming treatments. While modern innovation is important, traditional Arabian hospitality is still the essence of the service provided.

Continuing the traditions of ancient Arabia, The Spa's hammam rituals offer a unique purification experience. With its very own hammam, The Spa provides an insight into ancient Arabian traditions and guests can try this bathing custom as it has been performed throughout Arabia for centuries. The spa menu gives a choice between the 60-minute Traditional Hammam Cleansing or the 90-minute Royal Hammam Ritual.

Facials, body massages and wraps are also part of the extensive treatment menu. The Spa offers three facial treatment ranges for men and women: the anti-ageing facial range, the advanced performance range, and the skin-specific range. Each uses a combination of Elemis products with active plant ingredients and specific massage

sequences, which Elemis is renowned for. Combined with invigorating eye treatments, these personalized facial treatments will leave the skin visibly radiant.

With an exotic body wrap, one can drift off into a state of total relaxation. Slathered with a blend of special oils and completely enveloped in a warm wrap, this therapy improves skin tone and texture and helps to detoxify. The Aroma Spa Ocean Wrap, the Exotic Frangipani Body Nourishing Wrap, and the Exotic Coconut Rub and Milk Wrap are all tailored to indulge the senses and cleanse the body, leaving the skin beautifully soft and smooth.

Also on the spa menu are massages drawn from Bali, Japan and Thailand. There are two styles of Elemis body massages—Deep Tissue or Well-Being— to choose from, along with a choice of essential oil, which create a treatment tailored to specific needs. Afterwards, in the majlis, guests can savour the calming effects of the spa experience while enjoying breathtaking views over the Arabian Gulf.

It is possible to return to the golf course, or go sailing, or windsurfing, or horseback riding, or play tennis and much more. Privacy, relaxation and unmatched facilities are what you can expect at this five-star property which is also one of 'The Leading Hotels of the World'.

THIS PAGE (FROM TOP): One of the resort's three swimming pools so close to the beach; the Spa's Jacuzzi is great for pre-treatment relaxation.
OPPOSITE (CLOCKWISE FROM TOP): A massage at The Spa is tailor-made, you can choose from the Balinese, Japanese or Thai versions and either a deep tissue massage or a gentler well-being body massage, the choice of essential oil is also left up to you; the ladies' majlis is a great place to relax and re-adjust after your treatment; Arabian tradition and hospitality ensure an authentic experience.

Spa Statistics

TYPE OF SPA
Resort Spa

SPA AREA
900 sq m (9,700 sq ft)

FACILITIES
10 single treatment rooms; 1 ladies' majlis, 1 relaxation lounge; 1 Jacuzzi, 2 invigorating showers; 1 sauna, 1 steam room, 1 traditional hammam; 1 hair and beauty salon; 1 fully equipped gymnasium; 3 temperature-controlled swimming pools (1 saltwater pool), 1 outdoor children's pool; 9-hole golf course, 4 floodlit tennis courts, 1 squash court, 1 badminton court; 1 spa boutique

SIGNATURE TREATMENTS
Traditional Hammam Cleansing, Royal Hammam Ritual

OTHER TREATMENTS AND THERAPIES
Anti-ageing treatments, anti-cellulite treatments, back treatments, body scrubs, body wraps, bust treatments, facial treatments, firming and slimming treatments, hammam rituals, hand and foot treatments, hot stone therapies, massages, manicures/pedicures, pre-natal treatments, scalp massage, waxing

SPA CUISINE
Healthy, low-fat options and light calorie-reduced dishes are available at La Fontana restaurant

ACTIVITIES AND PROGRAMMES
Archery, beach volleyball, clay pigeon shooting, deep-sea fishing, golf academy, horse riding, sailing, water-skiing

SERVICES
Babysitting, children's club, complimentary herbal tea, fruit juice and fresh fruit, gift certificates, skincare consultation, spa consultation

LANGUAGES SPOKEN BY THERAPISTS
English, Arabic, French, Russian

ADMISSION
Open to staying and non-staying guests. Priority is given to staying guests. Guests under 16 years of age are not allowed in The Spa.

CONTACT
Jebel Ali Golf Resort + Spa
PO Box 9255
Dubai
United Arab Emirates
T +971 4 883 6000
F +971 4 883 5543
E jagrs@jaihotels.com
W www.jebelali-international.com

Six Senses Spa at Madinat Jumeirah

DUBAI, UNITED ARAB EMIRATES

True to the Six Senses Spa philosophy, the spa at Madinat Jumeirah The Arabian Resort, has been designed as a contemporary sanctuary that ably adopts the rich culture of Arabia. The only Six Senses Spa in the Middle East, the spa draws upon the true opulence of the Arabian traditions of well-being and uses its beautiful surroundings to rejuvenate and revitalize all those who visit. The experience at the Six Senses Spa in Dubai is a remarkable one that will stay with you long after you have left.

Right from the start, welcomed by the gentle sounds of flowing water, the aroma of exotic fragrances and sand-coloured buildings against brilliant blue skies, this sensory journey begins. Spa guests travel along the labyrinth of paths and waterways on an abra—a traditional water taxi— which gracefully glides past the enchanting gardens, through the courtyards and into one of the 26 stand-alone individual and twin treatment rooms. With such an introduction, spa guests can unwind before

they have even arrived. Upon arrival is a personal therapist who is ready to cater for any need. This is the overwhelming entrance for every spa guest at the Six Senses Spa at Madinat Jumeirah, a truly luxurious entrance to the world of ancient Arabia.

With no extravagance spared, the spa has been carefully laid out as a water-bound sanctuary, a place for beauty, healing and rejuvenation. Each treatment studio is a small individual island retreat that is situated amidst swaying palm trees and a tropical landscaped paradise. Guests can luxuriate in the balconies that overlook the beautiful and private gardens, while outdoor treatment tents offer a unique taste of Arabia within the lush greenery of the courtyard gardens.

To achieve the Six Senses Spa mission, the spa menu is designed to create a unique and memorable experience and in this paradise, with treatments that focus on health, relaxation, beauty, stress release and recuperation from the frantic pace of everyday

life, it would be difficult not to reach their goal. The two primary senses of sight and sound are instantly sated with the spa's exclusive surroundings but it is not until treatment begins that the third primary sense is addressed. The massages, body treatments and therapies ensure that the sense of touch is well taken care of. The choice on the menu covers a wide variety. Internationally acclaimed treatments and therapies from both East and West, for both men and women, are all here and the variation ensures that absolutely everyone is catered for with over 100 treatments to choose from. From Swedish to Thai to Balinese massages, from head massages to foot reflexology, from body wraps to facial treatments, every treatment and therapy is unique and especially tailored for individual guests with each programme offering total relaxation and rejuvenation.

Whichever treatment, it is guaranteed that the spa products are of exceptional quality and purity. You will find three skincare brands at the Six Senses; the widely acclaimed Sodashi range produced in Australia, the exclusive aromatherapy range from London, and the extravagant Shiffa product range made locally in the UAE. All product ranges use natural ingredients and are based on the sciences of dermatology, alternative health and aromatherapy. Most importantly, these brands spare no expense to

ensure the optimal result. The nourishing properties of the natural ingredients found in all of their products are quickly absorbed and utilized by the deepest layers of the skin.

One of the Six Sense's most luxurious and extravagant face and body treatments is the Shiffa Planet Earth Core Treatment. Precious gems such as diamonds, rubies and even gold, silver and

THIS PAGE (FROM TOP): Arabian décor in the luxurious spa; the entrance to the spa, its clean lines evoke an instant sense of calmness.
OPPOSITE: Guests can lie back and take in the sights and sounds as they are taken to the Six Senses Spa by water taxi.

crystals are used quite differently here from the conventional way, though its purpose is still to enhance a woman's beauty. To prepare for the lavish treatment that follows, the body is first sprayed, according to need, with either the Shiffa gold, silver or crystal spray. Aromatic clays are then mixed with precious gems. The synergy of the two ingredients works its magic when it is applied to the different areas of the body. Once the clay has been scrubbed off, the experience is completed with a soothing massage. Here, the therapist will apply elite Shiffa massage oils to the body. The effects of the sumptuous and extravagant ingredients work to replenish and renew the body.

The incredible blend of ingredients in the Shiffa products includes precious gems and metals as they effectively treat stress, cellulite, rheumatism, eczema and many other ailments. With such luxurious pampering, the body is overcome with a sense of well-being and ultimate pampering.

Furthermore, this range is completely exclusive to the Six Senses Spa at Madinat Jumeirah.

Alternatively, the Shiffa Planet Earth Bath begins with light skin brushing to scrub away dead skin. Once prepared, the therapist will massage luxurious oils containing diamond, sapphire or emerald, into the body. Guests can then relax in a customized and clay-infused bath allowing the clay and body oil to work together on the skin.

Another signature treatment at the Six Senses Spa is the Velvet Nights treatment—a body massage fit for royalty—that awakens all the senses. This sensuous 120-minute treatment is infused with mystery and luxury and is inspired by the ancient stories of love and the beauty of Arabia. Treatment begins with a flower-infused bath, followed by a body cleansing that uses ancient Arabian techniques, as well as a scalp massage, and underwater back and shoulder pressure point massage. The next stage of the Velvet Nights experience entails a whole-body

scrub using an ancient recipe of nuts, fruits, flowers and oils to exfoliate the body. Once ready for the final stage, a heated aromatic body massage ensues. This concluding part of the treatment leaves the body completely soothed and the mind calm.

If a milk bath appeals, consider the Andalusian Bath treatment. Beginning with an aroma-steam, the treatment includes a purifying Andalusian paste which is applied to the body. Once cleansed and rinsed from the body, an Andalusian oil—made from the resin of a million jasmine petals—is massaged onto the skin. Guests are then led to an enticing luxury Andalusian milk bath where the head and shoulders are massaged as the skin soaks in the goodness from the milk. Finally, a hydrating body massage completes the treatment leaving guests completely relaxed and the body feeling toned, while the skin is newly soft and shiny.

One journey that begins before even entering the treatment room and continues long after the experience is another of Six Senses' signature treatments—the Sensory Spa Journey. A luxurious footbath, skin-renewing treats, warm towels and fresh fragrances are just the beginning. What follows is a truly non-traditional body aroma massage. It's a variation of the Indonesian-style four-handed massage where two therapists work in complete tandem. One therapist delivers long, smooth massaging strokes along the body, while the second works in perfect synchrony delivering a cleansing facial treatment and a stress-relieving scalp massage. This combination allows the mind to let go of stress and leads to a deep state of calm. Once complete, this total body and mind encounter does

not end at the treatment room. Guests are given a special spa gift to take home, enabling the memory of this unique experience to survive long after treatment has ended.

Drawing upon the ancient traditions of Arabia, the much-loved rose is used to make up another of Shiffa's exquisite range of treatments. Exclusive to the Six Senses Spa, Madinat Jumeirah, The Rose Heaven treatment uses the therapeutic properties of attar of rose. The luxurious 150-minute ritual encompasses a rose steam using rosewater and incense, followed by the Rose of Damascus luxury body polish, the 1001 Roses luxury milk bath, ending

THIS PAGE (FROM TOP): In the sunken treatment room, skilled Six Senses Spa therapists can administer traditional Thai and shiatsu massages; a Royal Suite at Mina A'Salam hotel.
OPPOSITE (CLOCKWISE FROM TOP): The Honeymoon Treatment Room allows couples to experience the spa together; one of the spa's massage treatments; guests can have their treatment outside among the swaying palm trees.

with an underwater massage and a full body massage that uses the precious Rose Bliss Balm. Considered the queen of essential oils, the complex attar of rose will ease the mind with its fragrance.

As these treatments show, the Six Senses Spa is no ordinary spa. A cut above the rest, it also offers alternative and energy treatments too. Take for instance the Crystal Healing of Atlantis experience. Based on the healing philosophy that crystals are not inanimate matter—rather they are energy in crystallized form—the specially trained therapist uses one of 15 unique methods during treatment. One method, for example, uses different crystals that are placed over the body and each crystal works to receive, store and transmit energy. The seven chakra points along the body are the crown, the third eye (between the eye), the throat, the heart, the solar plexus, the belly and the base, and there are specific crystals—each possessing different healing

THIS PAGE (FROM LEFT): The peaceful surrounds of the Six Senses Spa's wet area; every part of the spa's grounds is utilized, here the tranquil garden makes the perfect place to enjoy one of the soothing massages.
OPPOSITE (CLOCKWISE FROM TOP): The colour cocoon room where guests are treated by alternating lights; crystals are known for their healing power and are used to unblock as well as store energy; couples can enjoy a romantic spa break.

properties—for each point. Throughout this treatment, the body is provided with a gentle but powerful way to clear energy blockages. Whether physical, emotional or spiritual, the healing energy of the crystals works to balance and harmonize body, mind and spirit.

Another forward-thinking and holistic therapy available to spa guests at the Six Senses Spa is colour therapy. This alternative therapy is actually an ancient method of healing that can be traced back 2,500 years when it was first used in Egypt, China and India. Even in the lost kingdom of Atlantis it is said that special chambers existed where people would visit to take in the healing combination of natural light and crystal. It is believed that different colours vibrate at different frequencies and, using this knowledge, therapists work in the Six Senses Spa's colour cocoon room, with light and colour to restore and improve the emotional, physical and mental state. The colours are alternated inside the room and different colours are applied to the body.

Guests will want to give themselves plenty of time at the spa both before and after the treatment. Indeed, guests are encouraged to luxuriate in the steam room or sauna prior to the appointment. This will help to relax the body and mind, help circulation, clear the respiratory system and flush toxins out of the body through the skin. Be sure to drink plenty of water to replenish all the water loss and to optimize the treatment benefits.

Adults can be comforted that children are not left out. Again, a cut above the rest, the Six Senses Spa offers a Children's Menu. So, while parents are enjoying their relaxing spa treatment, the children can have a pedicure, manicure, a facial treatment or even a special children's massage. A visit to this spa is a real treat for the whole family.

Other first-class facilities at the spa are also at your disposal. Showers, make-up rooms, Jacuzzi and plunge pool, wet relaxation areas and even a ladies semi-private majlis staffed by women, are available to make sure that those who arrive leave the spa looking their best. Having a manicure and pedicure, as well as getting your hair done at the hair salon adds to the final flourish.

Every detail towards your wellness is thought through at Six Senses, even after you leave the spa. Should you want to keep a slice of your experience at Six Senses, you can. Whether you want to pamper yourself in the comforts of your own home, or as a souvenir to loved ones upon your return, you can purchase the products used at the spa. Products by Sodashi, Shiffa and Aromatherapy Associates are available at the spa boutique.

The sense of smell satiated, the sense of touch soothed, the sense of sight sharpened. At the Six Senses Spa at Madinat Jumeirah, your sense of taste is well taken care of as well. Once you've nourished your skin, it's time to nourish your body within. If who we are is what we eat, then it is only befitting that a day of wellness includes a visit to the Senses Restaurant. A reflection of the spa philosophy of holistic wellness for body and mind, the restaurant aptly uses only fresh and natural produce, creatively and deliciously served. Many dishes listed on the menu can be found in the spa's very own Six Senses cookbook—a collection of mouth-watering dishes from the Six Senses Spa family around the globe. In keeping with the relaxed Six Senses atmosphere, the restaurant's environment of casual beauty makes it a

perfect finalé to a day of rewarding yourself. Outside of the spa, the resort offers an amazing variety of cuisines from Asian to Italian, from Moroccan to Moorish; all tastebuds are catered for.

Madinat Jumeirah or 'City of Jumeirah' also allows you therapy of another kind—retail therapy. Souk Madinat Jumeirah is an authentic bazaar-like retail experience with 75 shops, 23 bars, cafés and restaurants offering an eclectic mix of international cuisine. Shoppers can wonder through the meandering pathways where they will find open-fronted shops and intimate galleries that spill onto the paved walkways, offering unique brands and crafted quality goods. Soak in the sounds of craftsmen and women at work as the sweet aromas of delicious food and drink titillate the taste buds from the nearby cafés and restaurants.

40 hectares (99 acres) of landscaping and gardens provide cool and natural comfort all around. Should guests wish to expand their shopping experience, Madinat Jumeirah is conveniently located just 10 minutes away from shopping malls. You can reach these local amenities using the resort's exclusive limousine service.

Any time spent at Madinat Jumeirah is guaranteed to be the most luxurious and a truly unforgettable experience. Furthermore, voted the Best Spa in the Middle East for 2005 by readers of *Spa Finder* worldwide, it is clear that the Six Senses Spa is the perfect setting in which to balance the senses and discover that elusive sixth sense. For the sixth is only experienced when all of the five primary senses are elevated beyond expectation, which is exactly what you can expect at Madinat Jumeirah and Six Senses Spa.

Spa Statistics

TYPE OF SPA
Resort Spa

SPA AREA
6,700 sq m (72,120 sq ft)

FACILITIES
24 single indoor treatment villas, 2 double indoor treatment villas, 2 outdoor pavilions, 1 colour cocoon room; 1 consultation room; 1 meditation room, 1 relaxation room; 1 watsu pool, 1 cold plunge room, 1 reflexology pool; 1 sauna, 1 steam room, hammam; hair salon; 1 gymnasium

SIGNATURE TREATMENTS
Jet Lag Recovery, The Sensory Spa Journey, Time is Precious Day Rituals

OTHER TREATMENTS AND THERAPIES
Anti-ageing treatments, aromatherapy, ayurveda, Bach Flower Remedies, baths, body scrubs, body wraps, facial treatments, flotation, hair treatments, hand and foot treatments, holistic treatments, hot stone therapies, Indonesian therapies, jet-lag treatments, lymphatic drainage massage, manicures/pedicures, massages, reflexology, salon services, scalp treatments, Thai therapies, waxing

PROVISIONS FOR COUPLES
Couple suite

SPA CUISINE
Senses Restaurant serves only fresh and healthy dishes

ACTIVITIES AND PROGRAMMES
Camel rides, wildlife drives, dune drives, archery, falconry, horse rides, personal fitness programmes

SERVICES
Consultations, customized bridal packages, day-use rooms

LANGUAGES SPOKEN BY THERAPISTS
English

ADMISSION
Membership not required

CONTACT
Six Senses Spa
Madinat Jumeirah
PO Box 75157
Dubai
United Arab Emirates
T +97 1 4366 6818
F +97 1 4366 6800
E sixsensesspa@jumeirah.com
W www.jumeirah.com

One&Only Royal Mirage, Dubai Residence & Spa

DUBAI, UNITED ARAB EMIRATES

One&Only Royal Mirage is considered one of Dubai's most stylish beach resorts. From the outside the resort appears as a scene from a fairy tale—its cluster of reddish-brown buildings contrasting against the aquamarine waters of the Arabian Gulf, its lush landscaped gardens and streams of meandering water features, all lend themselves to an interesting blend of fantasy and Arabian tradition.

Within this dreamlike oasis sits the impressive Health & Beauty Institute. Its stunning Arabian-style architecture, complete with towering domes, carved arches and intricate design, create a picturesque landscape. In this setting, it comes as no surprise that indulgence and pampering are key.

Guests can wander onto the upper floors of the stand-alone spa building, where they will reach a centre for well-being; where the ornate reception of the Givenchy Spa awaits. Givenchy Spas have gathered renown in the spa world with their sister spas in Mauritius and France. Now, the name synonymous with elegance and luxury, this is exactly what guests can expect within the 12 private treatment rooms, including one exclusive suite for private consultations.

The Givenchy Spa's philosophy is simple: beauty stems from an inner sense of well-being. To this end, the spa aspires to achieve harmony and self-fulfilment through its range of luxurious treatments and cosmetic products. There is a treatment that caters to every single need for the whole body. Guests can choose from an extensive menu of facial treatments, massages and body wraps and scrubs, as well as foot reflexology.

For those who can't decide which treatment to choose, the spa's signature treatment is a good place to start. Simply named Exclusively Givenchy, it is the ultimate combination of three different body treatments that help to leave the skin feeling soothed, rejuvenated and hydrated. To prepare the body, the treatment begins with a body scrub to exfoliate and oxygenate the skin. For the second stage of the treatment, a deep bath is prepared, filled with specially selected Givenchy oils that will rejuvenate the skin. Then comes the grand finalé—a

hydrating wrap. Here, the body is covered with Swisscare Moisturising Bath. This will hydrate the skin, while you relax on a dry flotation bed and are simultaneously massaged at key points by multiple pressure jets. The result is perfectly refined skin and a wonderfully relaxed body.

You may be in the heart of Arabia, but the spa menu includes treatments from all around the world. The Canyon Love Stone Therapy feels as romantic as it sounds. Collected from the rivers of the American West, these beneficial, therapeutic stones are combined with draining oils that have been specially formulated by Givenchy, to provide a truly memorable treatment. The massage involves gliding the smooth, pure and warm surfaces of the stones over the body. The gentle but deep movements of the therapist's able hands create a feeling of total relaxation and well-being.

The spa treatments rely heavily on the use of Givenchy's luxurious cosmetic products. Facial treatments make up a large part of the menu and it's recommended that guests begin with the Preparatory Treatment. This deep cleansing facial is highly recommended and can be adjusted for all skin types. Firstly, the experienced therapists cleanse the face and gently exfoliate to remove any dull surface skin cells, after which, the skin is gently warmed by a massage and steam, readying it for the gentle extraction of any impurities. What follows is a nourishing facial mask selected specifically and suited for each individual skin type. This treatment works to oxygenate the skin, stimulate micro-circulation and revitalize the complexion.

Once the treatment has ended, guests are left with a sense of tranquillity that continues on throughout the day. The Givenchy Spa's resting area is a great space for your transition to the world outside. Its décor and creature comforts—complete with an organic juice bar—ensures that guests step out feeling radiant and rejuvenated.

For something a little more traditional, guests should venture to the lower floor of the Health & Beauty Institute. Here an authentic Oriental Hammam awaits. The warmth and steam permeates

THIS PAGE (CLOCKWISE FROM TOP LEFT): Arabian detail at the hammam; the majestic architecture of the Residence & Spa; Givenchy Spa's luxurious relaxation area; the rooftop of the stunning Arabian Court.
OPPOSITE: The traditional Oriental Hammam sits on the lower floor of the Health & Beauty Institute, guests can luxuriate in its soothing steam chambers.

the air to raise the body temperature and stimulate blood flow. Guests can relax in the warm marble seats as the space is filled with the soothing scent of eucalyptus. Alternatively, guests can lie on the traditional heated marble slab whilst being scrubbed and massaged by the experienced staff. Also in the lower floor complex are two steam rooms, two Jacuzzis, two private massage rooms, a plunge shower to cool off and a whirlpool, all nestled within the expansive resting area of the hammam.

Architecturally, the Hamman & Spa is a sight to behold. Majestic marble floors flow from room to room, highlighting the shiny blue mosaic tiles on the

walls. High domed ceilings and regal archways lead you into the inner sanctum of luxurious indulgence. In these beautiful and serene settings, traditional massages are administered.

A health and beauty institute would not be complete without a fitness centre. The fully-equipped gymnasium at the Residence & Spa has both indoor and outdoor exercise areas. So, for those looking for more interesting ways to raise the endorphin levels, there is a comforting range of choice. And, in keeping with its function as beauty provider, the Health & Beauty Institute also has a Ladies' and Gentlemen's Hair Salon. What's more, in order to ensure total privacy, there are dedicated operating hours for both ladies and gentlemen.

Other activities available to resort guests include an exhilerating desert safari. There is also a multitude of water sports at your disposal, from windsurfing to scuba diving, from snorkelling to water-skiing. There is even the option of experiencing some exciting deep-sea fishing excursions in the Gulf waters. Of course, golf is high on the agenda at this resort. Just minutes away are five spectacular courses that challenge golfers of all abilities.

The Health & Beauty Institute lies within the elegant entrance courtyard of the Residence & Spa at One&Only Royal Mirage, one of the 'Leading Small Hotels of the World'. This intimate sanctuary is a cluster of Arabian-styled private residences with only 18 suites and 32 Prestige Rooms. It has been created with the finest detailing and all suites have an amazing view of the sea, with their own private balconies or garden patios. With such style and impeccable spa service there is not much more the spa-goer could ask for.

Spa Statistics

TYPE OF SPA
Resort Spa

SPA AREA
2,000 sq m (21,530 sq ft)

FACILITIES
12 indoor treatment rooms; 1 consultation room, 1 relaxation room; 1 whirlpool; 2 steam rooms, 1 hammam; 1 ladies' hair salon, 1 men's hair salon; 1 gymnasium; 3 outdoor swimming pools; 3 tennis courts; 1 spa boutique

SIGNATURE TREATMENTS
Exclusively Givenchy

OTHER TREATMENTS AND THERAPIES
Aromatherapy, baths, body scrubs, body wraps, facial treatments, firming and slimming treatments, hot stone therapies, hydrotherapy, lymphatic drainage massage, massages, reflexology

SPA CUISINE
Juice bar at the spa

ACTIVITIES AND PROGRAMMES
Desert safari, fishing excursions, golf, sailing, scuba-diving, snorkelling

SERVICES
Babysitting, childcare

LANGUAGES SPOKEN BY THERAPISTS
English

ADMISSION
Exclusively for resort guests

CONTACT
One&Only Royal Mirage
P.O. Box 37252
Dubai
United Arab Emirates
T +971 4 399 9999
F +971 4 399 9998
E info@oneandonlyroyalmirage.ae
W www.oneandonlyresorts.com

Park Hyatt Dubai

DUBAI, UNITED ARAB EMIRATES

On the banks of the Dubai Creek and the world-famous Dubai Creek Golf Course, a sanctuary of luxury and tranquillity awaits. Here, time is not the essence; exclusivity and well-being take precedence. This is the Park Hyatt Dubai with its own exclusive Park Spa Rooms and luxurious day spa, Amara.

Just minutes from Dubai's world-class shopping and prime business districts, the hustle and bustle of the urban jungle is left outside the gates of this retreat. Once inside, guests are transported into a completely different world. Inspired by the rich culture and heritage of the region, the architecture of Park Hyatt Dubai seamlessly blends the Moorish and Mediterranean influences. Yet, this 225-room waterfront resort is fitted with all of the latest contemporary solutions for the modern business and leisure traveller.

The most unique feature of this urban sanctuary must be its eight Park Spa Rooms. It is the first and only hotel in Dubai to offer exquisitely furnished residential spa rooms—the ultimate in pampering. The Spa Rooms are complete with facilities enabling a premium well-being experience without having to ever leave the privacy of the suite. Each has its own private steam room, treatment area and private outdoor terrace. They are even equipped with specially designed multi-purpose treatment chairs, which can be used for a facial treatment, manicure, pedicure or a reflexology treatment.

Every detail of the Park Spa Room evokes a sense of luxury and well-being. In each of these rooms, an authentic Turkish kehsa exfoliating glove and hand-made pure olive pit oil soap are provided. Guests can have their very own traditional Turkish

bath to thoroughly cleanse the body, to remove dead skin cells and revive circulation. An aromatherapy body oil massage to soothe and moisturize the skin, concludes this soothing time-honoured ritual.

Handpicked professional therapists from the resort's day spa are at hand to provide the perfect indulgent ritual, in the privacy of these Spa Rooms. The rituals begin with an aromatic steam hammam. Guests can breathe in the aromas of essential oils that will gently lull the mind and body into total relaxation. The Shiffa Arabian Rose Hammam Ritual, for example, starts with a rose-essence steam. Step out of the hammam and into the private treatment area with its own built-in massage table. The ambient lighting, strategically-placed candles and soothing tunes set the scene for the next step in this exclusive spa experience, which continues with a nourishing rose body mask and scalp massage. This two-hour spa ritual closes with a massage using organic Arabian rose balm, leaving a lasting feeling of an Arabian fairy tale.

Honeymooners may prefer a more sensual ritual, the Rasul Ceremony, inspired by ancient harem rituals. Three different kinds of rare organic mud help to detoxify, heal and exfoliate the skin, when applied to specific areas of the body. Sea salt is applied over the mud during the aromatherapy

steam bath to ensure complete cleansing of the skin. What follows is a body massage using oils that gives this ritual a unique purifying and rejuvenating effect.

To complete the luxurious spa experience, guests can enjoy dinner on their own private outdoor terrace and continue to savour the peace and calm, while watching the scarlet sun set over the Creek.

Meanwhile, other hotel guests and local clientele can experience the same quality spa experience at the Amara day spa. With its own entrance, both privacy and tranquillity are promised in any one of its eight exclusive luxury suites each with their own outdoor terrace.

THIS PAGE (CLOCKWISE FROM TOP): A Park Spa Room featuring a massage table, steam room and treatment chair, making any spa break completely private; the two-storey Traiteur Restaurant offers modern European cuisine with wine from its vast wine cellar; one of Amara day spa's luxurious treatment suites.
OPPOSITE: The Amara lounge and pool sit majestically among the palm trees.

Besides using Europe's finest treatments and therapies, the spa products at Amara also include indigenous Arabian touches. Exclusive to Amara, the Anne Semonin range uses the vital forces of fresh herbs, plants and seaweeds to awaken the senses with unique formulations personalized for individual skin types. Shiffa, meaning 'healing' in ancient Arabic, is the world's premier organic aromatherapy line. Its exquisite therapies reflect ancient Arabian beauty philosophies through the use of pure and precious oils. Also an exclusive range, Carita—a highly effective anti-ageing skincare line—combines phytotherapy products, specialized massage techniques and exclusive pro lift technology to instantly lift and rejuvenate.

An extensive menu of spa treatments—all of which promise a superb result—leave clients spoilt for choice. For example, the five-hour Amara Ultimate Indulgence makes for a well-deserved treat. It begins with a 30-minute salt and pepper scrub to ready the skin for a regenerating body envelopment. After this revitalizing treatment, the next hour is spent on an aromatherapy body massage that leaves a calming and relaxing effect. The pampering continues with an Indian head massage. Drawing from the time-honoured Asian technique, this is a gentle but stimulating massage for the neck, shoulders and head.

Finally, the Amara Ultimate Indulgence ends with a 90-minute Carita Anti-Age Pro Lift Facial Treatment. This instant 'non-surgical' facelift is the secret behind many beautiful celebrity faces. Combining Carita's skincare rage and unique drainage massage techniques, this signature facial treatment counteracts and repairs the effects of time, using the exclusive 'Pro Lift' technology. With Carita's renowned Renovateur exfoliation and lifting, the skin appears well-rested, with a healthy radiance, smooth contours and redefined skin tone. Given the five wonderful hours of pampering, a 30-minute relaxation is advised to fully benefit from the whole experience at the end of it all.

For the energetic, plunge into Amara's 25-metre (82-foot) swimming pool. It is indeed stunning with a series of palm islands built within it. The hotel also offers a fully-equipped fitness studio and the Carita Salon for ladies and gentlemen. Those looking to tee off can do so at the international-standard golf facility within the complex, operated by Dubai Golf.

Right in the heart of the cosmopolitan business and leisure hub of the Middle East, Amara at Park Hyatt Dubai is the ideal retreat to stimulate the senses and soothe body, mind and soul.

Spa Statistics

TYPE OF SPA
Day Spa

SPA AREA
2,000 sq m (21,530 sq ft)

FACILITIES
8 Park Spa Rooms each with massage table, beauty treatment room, and steam room; 8 treatment rooms in Amara Day Spa; hammam, rasul; outdoor swimming pool; gymnasium; international-standard golf facility with driving range

SIGNATURE TREATMENTS
Amara Ultimate Indulgence, The Executive Rejuvenating and Balancing Ritual

OTHER TREATMENTS AND THERAPIES
After-sun care, anti-ageing treatments, aromatherapy, baths, body scrubs, body wraps, facial treatments, hot stone therapies, manicures/pedicures, massages, reflexology

ACTIVITIES AND PROGRAMMES
Fishing, golf, sailing

SERVICES
Babysitting

LANGUAGES SPOKEN BY THERAPISTS
English, Arabic, French

ADMISSION
Open to staying and non-staying guests

CONTACT
Park Hyatt Dubai
PO Box 2822
Dubai
United Arab Emirates
T +971 4 602 1234
F +971 4 602 1235
E dubai.park@hyattintl.com
W www.dubai.park.hyatt.com

The Health Club & Spa at Shangri-La

DUBAI, UNITED ARAB EMIRATES

The impressive 200-metre (656-feet), 43-storey Shangri-La Hotel, Dubai, is centrally located amongst the gleaming skyscrapers on Sheikh Zayed Road. Once you step away from the hustle and bustle outside, what lies within this five-star hotel is a haven of complete luxury and comfort—The Health Club & Spa at Shangri-La. Located on Level 4 of the hotel, the spacious and professionally-equipped Spa focuses on the overall well-being of its guests by embracing a holistic approach to vitality, fitness and beauty. The aim is to leave guests feeling relaxed, rejuvenated and revitalized both in body and in mind.

Inspired by ancient and traditional Asian healing philosophies, the extensive treatment menu has been inspired by the holistic concept of restoring balance and harmony. The signature treatment is the popular Chi Balance Massage, which comprises a unique blend of Asian techniques that encourages the flow of vital energy (or chi) to either strengthen and rejuvenate or calm and relax the body. Massage styles, including the acupressure option, can all be adjusted to suit individual needs in order to balance yin and yang and harmonize the flow of chi.

For a more gentle and sensual treatment, the Aroma Vitality Massage is the perfect choice. It brings together aromatherapy, shiatsu and reflexology with oriental essential oils. As such it is designed to boost the body's vital energy.

With the Futuresse Deluxe Body Treatment, the fascinating effect of the Lotus Regeneration Pearls is felt with the luxurious Lotus Silk Pack that relaxes the body and leaves the skin velvety soft. The Biodroga Milk and Honey Wrap is a cocktail of active ingredients which improves the skin's elasticity and firms the contours of the body.

Spa Statistics

TYPE OF SPA
Hotel Spa

SPA AREA
4,100 sq m (44,130 sq ft)

FACILITIES
9 treatment rooms (separate ladies' and gentlemen's facilities); 1 Jacuzzi, 5 plunge pools; 2 saunas, 2 steam rooms; hair salon and barber; gymnasium, movement studio; 1 squash court, 1 tennis court; 1 resort-style outdoor swimming pool; spa boutique

SIGNATURE TREATMENTS
Aroma Vitality Massage, Biodroga Treatments, Chi Balance Massage, Futuresse Treatments

OTHER TREATMENTS AND THERAPIES
Anti-ageing treatments, Asian therapies, body scrubs, body wraps, chi treatments, facial treatments, hand and foot treatments, massages, reflexology

LANGUAGES SPOKEN BY THERAPISTS
English

ADMISSION
Open to staying and non-staying guests

CONTACT
Shangri-La Hotel, Dubai
Sheikh Zayed Road
P.O Box 75880
Dubai
United Arab Emirates
T +971 04 405 2441/2447
F +971 04 343 8886
E sldb.spa@shangri-la.com
W www.shangri-la.com

To complete the extensive menu, The Health Club & Spa at the Shangri-La offers body scrubs and a variety of soothing therapies, such as the Nature Wrap. This treatment uses the organic compound, benzoin—also known as bitter almond-oil camphor—which has been combined with various therapeutic oils and white clay, to help dispel toxins and draw impurities from the body. The result is a lighter skin tone and a 'good as new' glow.

For those wishing to take their spa experience home with them, the Spa has its very own exclusive line of products on offer at the Spa boutique. The luxury skincare line, developed in Australia, uses all-natural ingredients and was especially designed for Shangri-La Hotels and Resorts worldwide. The Health Club & Spa at Shangri-La Hotel, Dubai, also uses the Spa range, Biodroga, which combines the very latest in special product technology and advanced techniques for extraordinary results in both facial and body care.

What sets this spa apart from others, though, is its excellent standard of service. The Spa's therapists have extensive knowledge of a wide range of specialized Eastern and cosmopolitan therapies, which are all available upon request. So, if there is something in particular that a guest has in mind, all they need to do is ask.

THIS PAGE (FROM TOP): Clean, minimalist lines decorate the Spa's reception area; Tibetan chimes are used to awaken the senses after a relaxing treatment.
OPPOSITE (CLOCKWISE FROM TOP): The multiple benefits of a plunge pool vary from complete relaxation to an anti-inflammatory effect on the skin; all treatments are administered in the stylish, fully-equipped treatment rooms; the impressive outdoor swimming pool appeals to all sun-worshippers.

Dalouk Spa Sharjah Ladies Club

SHARJAH, UNITED ARAB EMIRATES

An atmosphere of serenity and well-being is evident as soon as you enter Dalouk Spa at the Sharjah Ladies Club. Senses are piqued as the aromas of Arabia waft through the air and the glint of the rich mosaic of marine colours catches your eye. The spa epitomizes luxury and refinement.

The approach at Dalouk Spa is a holistic one where both body and soul are treated. This total wellness philosophy ensures guests will look great and feel great too. In keeping with this concept, the Spa also believes in Mother Nature and is proud to be one of the few spas in the world to use only products that are 100 per cent pure and natural.

Sourced from Living Nature and Aromatherapy Associates, they are guaranteed to be truly organic, GM-free and preserved without artificial agents; Dalouk Spa endeavours to provide its guests with only the best that nature has to offer.

If a massage is called for, Dalouk Spa is the right place. The massage menu features a huge variety. With aromatherapy, hot stone, holistic and shaitsu massages, an Oriental foot massage and Chinese bodywork therapy, guests can choose from the spa's extensive range that draws from the healing wisdom of various cultures and traditions including, of course, the traditions of Arabia.

The Honey & Orange Massage is deliciously refreshing, but it is the Saffron Body Polish that tops the list. Honey, almonds, fine-grain rice, rosewater and saffron are the ingredients of this delightful treatment. For 40 minutes, one can relax as these traditional Arabian ingredients are made into a luxurious paste and massaged onto the body, exfoliating the skin, leaving it luxuriously soft and smooth. This is followed by a body wrap and a simultaneous head massage to ensure you completely unwind. By the end of this exquisite treatment, the body will literally glow with wellness, and you'll feel good from inside out.

A number of signature treatments at Dalouk Spa are good enough to eat. Take for example, the Honey & Cucumber Facial—ingredients for a great salad, and so too a moisturising facial treatment. Guests can indulge in their own uniquely tailored facial treatment designed specifically for their own skin type using only natural ingredients. The Organic Living Nature Facial is another must-try and is available nowhere else in the Gulf. Before the facial treatment begins, trained therapists make a thorough skin analysis to determine skin type and decide on the correct course of action. A deep cleansing peel follows, leaving the skin smooth, clean and ready for extraction. Next, a mask is applied to soothe the skin, while a special massage for the face, scalp, décolleté, neck and shoulders helps to drain the lymphatic system, leaving the skin with a newly healthy and radiant glow.

Dalouk Spa has its very own purpose-built Thalassotherapy Centre, the only spa in the Gulf to own one, making it unique and one of the best. Greek for 'sea' and 'cure', thalassotherapy refers to all treatments that use seawater and sea-based ingredients. Since ancient times, the sea has been renowned for its curative powers and health benefits.

OPPOSITE: Dalouk Spa provides a safe haven to while away the hours in the kind of luxury demanded by ladies of sophistication and good taste.
THIS PAGE (CLOCKWISE FROM TOP LEFT): A crystal massage is incorporated into all the spa's 'Living Nature' facial treatments, the 'anti wrinkle' effects of the crystals are fantastic; herbal tea to complement any treatment; the nourishing Saffron Body Polish ingredients, all the products used are 100 per cent natural, GM-free and not tested on animals; for light, fresh and wholesome food with a Middle Eastern and Mediterranean style, visit the gourmet restaurant, Lafeef.

And having seawater right by its doorstep, it is only natural that Dalouk takes full advantage of it and its healing properties. The thalassotherapy pool treats ailments ranging from poor circulation, rheumatism, muscle pain and obesity to lymphatic and joint articulation problems and chronic fatigue.

It is easy to spend a whole day at the Sharjah Ladies Club. Sun-worshippers can delight on the beach outside as they soak in the rays while the aquamarine waters of the Arabian Gulf lap on the shore. Not to be left out, fitness fanatics can enjoy a couple of laps in the Olympic-size swimming pool or a run on the treadmill in the fitness centre. There is even an ice-skating rink. After all the exertion, guests are able to wind down with a relaxing Dalouk Holistic Massage, Organic Cell Renewal Facial or a glorious underwater massage at Dalouk Spa to ease those tired muscles.

For lunch or dinner after a full day at the spa, a quick visit to the neighbouring restaurant, Lafeef, provides a welcome relief to any hunger pangs. It offers a healthy menu featuring an eclectic mix of Middle Eastern and Mediterranean fare with an

emphasis on light, fresh food and wholesome ingredients. Just sitting at the glassed beachfront restaurant alone, with a stunning view of the sea, is enough to ease the soul.

At Sharjah Ladies Club, your every need is taken care of, including your children's. Spa guests can have complete peace of mind as the child-friendly staff of keep the little ones entertained. While mum enjoys some pampering, the children will be entertained with playing games, drawing, watching videos, or even building sandcastles on the private beach. Without doubt they will have a great time, leaving any busy mother to totally relax and enjoy her spa treatment.

With the bevy of activities and facilities offered at the Sharjah Ladies Club, guests can rest assured that it is a private haven for women, a place for complete relaxation, and where a spa experience can be enjoyed at total ease.

Spa Statistics

TYPE OF SPA
Day Spa

SPA AREA
932 sq m (10,000 sq ft)

FACILITIES
6 treatment rooms; 1 relaxation room; 1 body wrap room; 1 Moroccan bath, 1 balneotherapy room, 1 thalassotherapy pool; 1 steam room; 1 beauty salon, library, TV room; 1 gymnasium, 1 aerobics studio, cycling studio, karate dojo, ballet studio; 2 outdoor pools (1 olympic-size, 1 leisure pool); 2 outdoor tennis courts, 1 indoor tennis court; ice-skating rink

SIGNATURE TREATMENTS
Complete Body De-Tox, Dalouk Holistic Massage, Honey & Orange Massage, Living Nature Organic Treatments, Photo Rejuvenation Facial, Saffron Body Polish

OTHER TREATMENTS AND THERAPIES
Anti-ageing treatments, anti-cellulite treatments, aromatherapy, body scrubs, body wraps, day packages, de-tox treatments, facial treatments, firming and slimming treatments, hand and foot treatments, hydrotherapy, jin shin jyutsu, manicures/pedicures, monthly therapeutic programmes, pre- and post-natal treatments, purifying back treatments, salon services, thalassotherapy, variable pulsed-light skin rejuvenation and hair removal, waxing

SPA CUISINE
Healthy, light meals available at Lafeef restaurant

ACTIVITIES AND PROGRAMMES
Aerobics, Arabic and English conversation classes, art classes, ballet classes, body balance, body combat, body pump, circuit training, dance aerobics, fabulous abs, fit teen, ice-skating, meditation, RPM, step aerobics, tae-bo, TBT, tennis and table tennis, yoga

SERVICES
Body composition analysis, fitness assessment, gift certificates, personal training, skincare consultations

LANGUAGES SPOKEN BY THERAPISTS
English, Arabic, Balinese, Chinese, Croatian, French, Italian, Tagalog

ADMISSION
For women over 16 only. Open to members of Sharjah Ladies Club and their guests. Day visitors welcome.

CONTACT
Sharjah Ladies Club
Sharjah
United Arab Emirates
T +971 6564 6663
F +971 6565 7799
E dalouk@sharjahladiesclub.com
W www.sharjahladiesclub.com

Spa Speak

A glossary of common spa, treatment and fitness terms. Variations may be offered, so it's best to check with the respective spas when you make your booking.

Abyhanga Gentle, rhythmic ayurvedic massage in which therapists work warm oil into the body to help enhance the immune system and encourage the removal of toxins.

Acupoints Points along the meridian channels where the life force—qi (Chinese), prana (Indian) and ki (Japanese)—accumulates. Also known as sên (Thai).

Acupressure Application of fingertip (and sometimes palm, elbow, knee and foot) pressure on the body's acupoints to improve the flow of qi throughout the body, release muscle tension and promote healing.

Acupuncture Ancient Chinese healing technique in which fine needles are inserted into acupoints along the body's meridians to maintain health and correct any imbalance that causes illness.

Aerobics Fitness routine that involves a series of rhythmic exercises usually performed to music. Promotes cardiovascular fitness, improves the body's use of oxygen, burns calories and increases endurance.

Aerobics studio Area used for floor exercises.

Affusion shower massage Massage given under a relaxing, rain-like, warm shower of water or seawater. Increases blood circulation.

After-sun treatment Treatment that soothes skin that has been over-exposed to the sun, and cools the over-heated body. May include a cooling bath and a gentle massage with a lotion of soothing ingredients such as cucumber and aloe vera.

Aikido Japanese martial art that uses techniques such as locks and throws, and focuses on using the opponent's own energy against himself.

Alexander Technique Therapy developed by Australian F M Alexander in the 1890s that retrains you to stand and move in an optimally balanced way. Helps reduce physical and psychological problems brought on by bad posture.

Algotherapy Use of algae in treatments such as baths, scrubs, wraps and skin care.

Anti-cellulite treatment Treatment that contours the body and reduces cellulite at various parts of the body.

Anti-stress massage Typically a 30-minute introductory massage, or one for those with limited time and who suffer from high levels of stress. Focuses on tension areas such as the back, face, neck and shoulders.

Aquaerobics Aerobic exercises performed in a swimming pool where the water provides support and resistance to increase stamina, and stretch and strengthen muscles.

Aquamedic pool Pool with specially positioned therapeutic jets for benefits such as relaxation and improving muscle tone.

Aromatherapy Ancient healing art that dates back to 4,500 BC. Refers to the use of essential oils from plants and flowers in treatments such as facials, massages, body wraps, foot baths and hydrobaths.

Aromatherapy massage Massage in which essential oils—either pre-blended or specially mixed for your needs—are applied to the body, typically with Swedish massage techniques.

Asanas Yoga postures.

Ashtanga A fast-paced form of yoga.

Aura An electromagnetic field or subtle body of energy believed to surround each living thing. Traditionally thought of as oval in shape and comprising seven layered bands. Its colour, shape, size and action are believed to reflect your physical, emotional, psychological and spiritual well-being.

Ayurveda Holistic system in India encompassing diet, massage, exercise and yoga.

Ayurvedic massage Massage performed by one or more therapists directly on the skin to loosen the excess doshas. Promotes circulation, increases flexibility, and relieves pain and stiffness. Applied with herbal oil.

Baby massage Infant massage that focuses on the special needs of newborns. Massage is used to relax, improve circulation and relieve common infant ailments. It also nurtures bonding between infant and parent when performed by the latter.

Bach Flower Therapies 38 flowers remedies, each associated with specific negative feelings, developed by Dr Edward Bach in the 1930s. The remedies are derived from solarized flowers that work on a vibrational level to effect emotional change. Flower therapies are also known as flower essences.

Back treatment Deep cleansing skin treatment for the back, neck and shoulders that removes impurities and excess oils, eases tension, and leaves the skin soft and smooth. Also known as clarifying back treatment or purifying back treatment.

Balinese boreh Traditional warming Balinese mask made from herbs and spices which improve circulation and skin suppleness. The paste is lightly applied to the body, which is then wrapped in a blanket. The spices produce a sensation of deep heat.

Balinese coffee scrub Exfoliating scrub in which finely ground Balinese coffee beans are applied to the skin.

Balinese massage Relaxing traditional massage of Bali that uses rolling, long strokes, and finger and palm pressure. Applied with oil.

Balneotherapy Water treatments that use hot springs, mineral water or seawater to improve circulation, restore and revitalize the body, and relieve pain and stress. Also an invigorating, re-mineralizing treatment for muscles that uses water jets and a localized massage in a tub with a special hose administered by a therapist.

Bath Soaking or cleansing the body in water that is typically infused with salt, flowers, minerals or essential oils. May serve as a prelude to, or conclude a treatment.

Bikram Hot yoga, where yoga is practised in room heated to 29°C-38°C (84°F–100°F).

Blisswork Deep tissue exercise that works to lengthen the body and seeks to restore it to its original design.

Blitz shower Standing body massage in which a high-pressure shower jet is directed at the body or specific parts of the body by a therapist who is about 3 metres away. Has a deep massaging effect, which increases circulation. Also known as douche au jet, jet blitz or jet massage.

Beauty treatment Treatment provided by spas to enhance beauty and overall well-being. Includes facial treatments, makeovers, manicures, pedicures and waxing.

Body bronzing Tanning treatment without the sun. May begin with a scrub to smooth the skin, which allows for an even tan.

Body composition analysis Evaluation of lean body mass to determine the percentage of body fat for the purpose of tailoring a nutrition and exercise programme.

Body mask Regenerating treatment in which the body is slathered with clay. The minerals in the clay—which may be mixed with essential oils—detoxify and hydrate the skin, leaving it refreshed and radiant.

Body scrub Exfoliating body treatment, using products such as salt or herbs, that removes dry, dead skin cells and improves blood circulation. Softens the skin and gives it a healthier glow. Often used for preparing the skin to receive the benefits of massages and wraps. Also known as body polish.

Body treatment General term that denotes treatments for the body.

Body wrap Treatment in which the body is wrapped in linen soaked in a herbal solution for about 20 minutes, and sometimes kept under a heated blanket. May be preceded by an application of fruit, herbs, mud or seaweed, and accompanied by a face, head and scalp massage. Detoxifies the system, soothes tired muscles and hydrates the skin.

Bodywork Therapeutic touching or manipulation of the body that uses massage or exercise to relax, ease tension and pain, and treat illnesses. May involve lessons in proper posture or movement. Some modes may treat both the body and mind.

Brush and tone Use of a loofah, special brush or rough cloth to rapidly brush the body to remove dead skin cells and impurities. Often used to prepare the body for treatments such as masks and bronzing. Also known as dry brushing.

Bust treatment Treatment to firm and tone the bust and décolleté.

Cardamom One of the oldest spices known, it is traditionally used as a medicinal aid for indigestion and flatulence, and commonly added to desserts, coffee, soaps, lotions and perfumes for its fragrance.

Chair massage Massage performed while seated on a specially designed massage chair. The chair is portable so the massage can be performed almost anywhere. The massage typically concentrates on the back, neck, scalp and shoulders.

Chakras The seven electromagnetic energy centres located along the spine that are associated with the flow of the body's subtle energy and which influence specific glands and functions within the body.

Champissage Head massage developed by blind Indian therapist Nehendra Mehta, who popularized his technique in London during the 1980s.

Chromatherapy Coloured light therapy, taken from the Greek word khroma, meaning light.

Chi nei tsang Internal organ massage that focuses on the abdominal area where stress, tension and negative emotions accumulate. Relieves illness, and releases negative emotions and tensions, bringing relief to the abdomen and vital energy to the internal organs. Eliminates toxins in the gastrointestinal tract, promotes lymphatic drainage and treats digestive problems such as irritable bowel syndrome, bloating and constipation.

Cold plunge pool Small pool filled with chilled water to stimulate blood and cool the body quickly, especially after a sauna.

Colour therapy Use of colour to bring about balance. Colour therapy can be admininstered using light, water, crystals, visualization, and food. It is believed that different colours vibrate at different rates. and each colour emits its own subtle energy. The body can be treated with the associated stones placed on the relevant chakra point.

Complementary therapy Health care system not traditionally utilized by conventional Western medical practitioners, and which may complement orthodox treatments. Also known as alternative therapy.

Cranial-sacral therapy A gentle touch therapy that evaluates and enhances the cranio-sacral system (comprising the membranes and fluid that surround and protect the brain and spinal cord) to restore balance, ease stress and enhance the body's self-healing process. The technique was developed in the mid-1970s by osteopathic physician John E Upledger.

Crème bath Hair and scalp conditioning treatment in which a rich cream is applied to the hair section by section. The hair may be steamed before being rinsed. May include a neck, scalp and shoulder massage.

Crystal and gem therapy A form of healing through the use of crystals and gemstones, which are believed to be able to transmit and receive energy, to modify thoughts, emotions and energy fields, thereby serving to restore balance in the body and amplify innate healing ability. Often performed with reiki and colour therapy. Most commonly used gems include gold, diamond, emerald, ruby and sapphire.

Cupping Treatment where small glass cups are attached to the skin by a vacuum that is created by placing a lit match inside each cup to burn the oxygen. The suction increases the circulation of the body's vital energy and blood.

Dance movement therapy Dance as a therapy, with or without music, to help those with emotional problems. The therapist may suggest movements and encourage the participants to innovate their own to express themselves.

Dancercise Aerobic exercise derived from modified modern dance steps and movements.

Date Fruit of the date palm—the 'tree of life' in Muslim legend—cultivated in Arabian culture for millennia as a prize source of nutrition and medicinal properties, such as disinfection in wound healing, skin regeneration and anti-ageing.

Dead Sea mud treatment Application of mineral-rich mud from the Dead Sea. Detoxifies the skin and body, improves cell metabolism and relieves rheumatic and arthritic pain.

Deep tissue massage Firm and deep massage using specific techniques to release tensions, blockages and knots that have built up over time. Believed to release emotional tension. May be adapted to a specific area of tension.

Do-in System of exercise resembling yoga postures that encourages physical and spiritual development. Balances the flow of energy through the meridian system.

Doshas In ayurveda, the three humours that make up the physical body. Also describes the three constitutional types.

Echocardiography Technique used for diagnosing cardiovascular illness by examining the heart and its vessels using non-invasive equipment.

Effleurage Long, even strokes in the direction of the heart which helps push along the flow of blood and lymph.

Endermologie Massage therapy using the Cellu M6 machine to reduce the appearance of cellulite and refine the figure.

Energy balancing A general term to describe a variety of practices aimed at balancing the flow of energy in and around the body. Practitioners generally try to remove blockages, and balance and amplify this energy flow.

EQ4 meridian testing Combination of traditional Chinese medicine, homeopathy, kinesiology, medical research and modern computing. A probe is applied to the acupoints to determine the areas that require treatment. It is believed that allergens, food and environmental stresses that weaken the body are reflected in energy levels that are higher or lower than normal.

Equilibropathy Treatment that encourages the body to function properly by relaxing tense muscle groups in order to regulate the body's systems and ensure they work together harmoniously. It begins with an examination of the spinal column and associated muscle groups to determine the cause of health problems and reveal asymptomatic illnesses. A modified acupuncture technique is then used to help release tense and knotted muscle groups. Breathing exercises are taught to stimulate the muscles to release tension and correct the body's structures.

Essential oils Oils, extracted from plants and flowers, that have specific characteristics that determine their use. They may be sedative or stimulating, and have antibacterial and therapeutic qualities. Usually inhaled or used in treatments such as massages, where they are absorbed by the skin.

Exfoliation Removal of dry, dead skin cells and impurities that impede oxygenation, using products such as salt or herbs, or techniques such as dry brushing.

Eyebrow shaping Grooming of the eyebrows, typically by tweezing, to suit the facial features.

Eye treatment Treatment that focuses on the delicate eye area, generally to combat signs of premature ageing, relieve tired eyes, and reduce puffiness and dryness.

Facial Treatment that cleanses and improves the complexion of the face using products that best suit a specific skin type. May include gentle exfoliation, steaming to open pores for extractions, application of a facial mask and moisturizer, and a facial massage. Types of facials include aromatic, oxygenating, whitening and deep cleansing facials.

Facial mask Cleansing facial treatment where products are applied on the face and left on for a period of time to cleanse pores and slough off dead skin.

Facial scrub Exfoliating face treatment that uses products with abrasive ingredients to remove dry, dead skin cells and improve blood circulation. Softens the skin and gives it a healthier glow.

Fig Fruit of the Ficus carica tree, native to the Middle East and Mediterranean and thought to be the world's first cultivated tree. The fruit is a rich source of simple sugars, minerals and fibre, while the leaves have been found to help stabilize blood sugar levels in the body.

Fitness facial for men Facial that addresses men's specific skin types and needs, including shaving rash. May include a face, neck and shoulder massage.

Flotation therapy Treatment where you float on salt and mineral water at body temperature in an enclosed flotation tank (also known as an isolation tank). The feeling of weightlessness, and the isolation from external sensations and stimuli provide a deep feeling of relaxation and sensory awareness. May be done in complete silence and darkness, or with music and videos. A two-hour treatment is said to be the equivalent of eight hours sleep.

Floral bath Flower-filled bath with essential oils.

Frankincense Aromatic gum resin from the North African Boswellia tree, formerly valued for ceremonial worship, embalming and fumigation. Forms a strong disinfectant when burned with other incense herbs.

Four-handed massage Massage performed in complete tandem by two therapists. Often uses a blend of massage techniques.

G5 vibro massage Deep vibrating massage using a G5 machine that relaxes, stimulates circulation and breaks down fatty deposits.

Glycolic facial Facial that uses glycolic acid to break down the bond which holds dry skin on to the face. Exfoliates the top layer, smoothes the skin and softens lines.

Golden spoons facial Facial treatment using alternating hot and cold 23-karat gold-plated spoons to open and close the pores. Stimulates circulation and helps the skin absorb creams and lotions.

Gommage Massage-like treatment using creams to cleanse and moisturize.

Gong fu Generic term for martial arts that originated in China.

Gymnasium Workout room with weights, and a range of high-tech cardio and variable resistance equipment.

Hair services Services for the hair, including cutting, styling, deep conditioning, hair colouring, and washing and blow drying.

Hammam Turkish steam bath using aromatherapy essences that cleanse, purify, and stimulate blood circulation. The typical Hammam consists of a series of interconnecting chambers and pools of varying temperatures; bathers can wander between rooms, starting from the coolest and moving to the hottest before completing their ritual in a cold plunge pool. In todays spas, it is usually part of an overall ritual that combines bathing with massage, scrubs and sometimes facials.

Hatha Common form of yoga, focuses on control through asanas and breathing techniques.

Hay diet Diet, devised by American physician Dr William Howard, that recommends carbohydrates are eaten at separate mealtimes from proteins and acidic fruit. Carbohydrates and proteins are not to be eaten within four hours of each other. Pulses and peanuts are not included in this diet.

Henna A dwarf shrub whose leaves are traditionally powdered to produce a pigment used for dying hair and tattooing the body and nails, their painted designs bearing different significances—from good health and fertility to wisdom and spiritual enlightenment. Believed to have healing and cooling properties, Henna has long been used to prepare concoctions for treating a myriad of ailments, from sun-induced headaches and rheumatism to jaundice and enlargement of the liver.

Herbal compress treatment Treatment where a heated muslin or cotton parcel of herbs and spices are placed on various parts of the body to relieve sore muscles, boost circulation and refresh the skin. The herbal packs are also used in place of hands to massage the body. Also known as herbal heat revival.

Herbal medicine Use of medicinal herbs and plant-based medicine to prevent and cure illnesses. Some healing systems, traditional Chinese medicine for instance, use mineral- and animal-based ingredients in herbal medicine. Herbal medicine is used by many complementary health disciplines including ayurveda, homeopathy, naturopathy, and Chinese, Indonesian and Japanese medicines. It may be prepared for internal and external uses through various forms such as pills, teas, oils or compresses. Also known as herbalism.

Herbal steam infusion Steaming with herbs. The heat, moisture and fragrance of the herbs help to open the pores and promote relaxation.

Herbal wrap Treatment where the body is wrapped in hot cloth sheets soaked in a herbal solution. Eliminates impurities, softens the skin, and detoxifies and relaxes the body.

Herbology Therapeutic use of herbs in treatments and diets.

High-impact aerobics Aerobics involving jumping, jogging and hopping movements where both feet loose contact with the ground.

Holistic approach Integrated approach to health and fitness that takes into account your lifestyle, and mental, physical and spiritual well-being.

Homeopathy Holistic health care practice, based on the concept of 'like cures like', that treats diseases by using minute doses of natural substances that in a healthy person would produce symptoms similar to what is already being experienced. The practice was developed by German physician Dr Samuel Hahnemann (1755-1843).

Honey A sweet viscous fluid processed by bees from nectar collected from flowers of plants. Traditionally used as an antiseptic for treating ulcers and wounds, and consumed to boost immunity as well as to soothe the throat, stressed skin and inflamed joints. (Bees also produce bee pollen, propolis and royal jelly, which share powerful health benefits.)

Hot plunge pool Pool of hot water that helps open the capillaries.

Hot spring Natural, sometimes volcanic, spring of hot mineral water.

Hot tub Wooden tub of hot or cool water to soak the body.

Hydrobath Bathtub with water jets that pummel all parts of the body. Seawater may be used, or the water may be infused with essential oils or mineral salts. Relaxes, and stimulates muscle tone and circulation.

Hydromassage Underwater massage in a hydrobath equipped with high-pressure jets and hand-manipulated hoses to stimulate the blood and lymphatic circulations.

Hydropool Pool fitted with various high-pressure jets and fountains.

Hydrotherapy Therapeutic use of water which includes baths, steam baths, steam inhalation, in- and under-water massage, soaking in hot springs, and the use of hot, cold or alternating shower sprays.

Indonesian massage Traditional massage of Indonesia that uses deep pressure and specially blended massage oils to ease tension and improve circulation.

Iridology Analysis of the marks and changes on the iris, which is divided into areas that are linked to specific body parts and functions, to diagnose a problem, or spot early signs of trouble, in order to recommend appropriate action.

Iyengar Form of yoga that focuses on symmetry and alignment. Props are commonly used.

Jamu Traditional Indonesian herbal medicine.

Javanese lulur Traditional fragrant scrub originating from the royal palaces of Java. A blend of powdered spices, including turmeric and sandalwood, is rubbed on to the body. After the vibrantly coloured paste dries, it is removed with a gentle massage. The skin is then moisturized with yogurt. The lulur is often used to clean and pamper the bride during the week leading up to her wedding.

Jet-lag treatment Treatment that specifically eases travel-associated aches, pains and stiffness, and helps the body to adjust to the new time zone.

Kanpo Japanese traditional herbal medicine. Less commonly used to refer to the Japanese traditional healing system.

Ki The life force that sustains the body. Known as qi in traditional Chinese medicine.

Kinesiology Use of fingertip pressure to locate weakness in specific muscles and diagnose a problem or asymptomatic illnesses. The fingertips are used to massage the appropriate points to disperse toxins and revitalize the flow of energy.

Kneipp baths Herbal or mineral baths of varying temperatures combined with diet and exercise. Kneipp therapy uses hot and cold hydrotherapy treatments to improve circulation.

Kundalini A form of yoga that combines chanting and breathing exercises with different asanas. Designed to awaken the body's kundalini energy.

Kur Course of daily treatments using natural resources, such as algae and thermal mineral water, used to re-mineralize and balance the body.

Labyrinth Ancient meditation tool in which a single winding path leads to a central goal and back out again. Walking it is a metaphor for journeying to the centre of understanding and returning with a broadened outlook.

Lap pool Swimming pool with exercise lanes. Standard lap pools are 25 metres in length.

Life coach counselling Counselling sessions that help to solve daily problems, develop harmony with the self and contribute to understanding life's natural philosophy.

Light therapy Use of natural or artificial light to heal see chromatherapy and colour therapy.

Lomi Lomi Massage originating in Hawaii that uses the forearms and elbows, rhythmical rocking movements, and long and broad strokes over the body.

Low-impact aerobics Form of aerobics with side-to-side marching or gliding movements which spare the body from excessive stress and possible injuries.

Lymphatic drainage massage Massage that uses a gentle pumping technique to stimulate lymphatic circulation, and thus reduce water retention and remove toxins. Lymph drainage can be achieved through manual massage or hydromassage. May be performed on the face and neck, or on the body.

Lymphobiology Treatment that combines a massage with an application of biological products to improve the skin's condition. Provides a radiant glow, reduces cellulite, restores hydration, controls acne, balances oily or dry skin, minimizes lines and wrinkles, and corrects post-surgical bruising and swelling.

Macrobiotics Diet that aims to balance foods by their yin-yang qualities and according to your needs.

Malay massage Traditional massage that uses pressure and long, kneading strokes. May be applied with herbal oil.

Manicure Treatment that beautifies the hands and nails. Hands are initially soaked and exfoliated with a scrub to remove dead skin cells, cuticles are groomed, and nails are trimmed and shaped. Nails may be buffed to a shine or coated with a polish. May include a hand massage.

Manuluve Hand and arm treatment comprising a scrub and heated seaweed massage.

Marine aerosol treatment Inhalation of ionic seawater mist to cleanse the respiratory system. Alleviates breathing problems caused by asthma or smoking.

Marma point massage Ayurvedic massage in which the marma points are massaged with the thumb or index fingers in clockwise circles. Focuses on the face, neck, scalp and shoulders.

Marma points The ayurvedic vital energy points. It's believed that the dysfunction of any marma point leads to illness.

Massage Therapy that uses manipulative and soft tissue techniques that are generally based on concepts of the anatomy, physiology and human function. Relaxes, creates a sense of well-being, eases strain and tension, mobilizes stiff joints, improves blood circulation, improves the digestive system, and encourages the removal of toxins from the body. Generally delivered by hand, though machines and high-powered water-jets are also used.

Masseur Male massage therapist.

Masseuse Female massage therapist.

Meditation Method of deep breathing, mental concentration and contemplation. During meditation, breathing, brain activity, and heart and pulse rates slow, encouraging the body to relax and achieve a greater sense of inner balance and peace. Relieves stress, removes pain and reduces blood pressure.

Meridians Pathways or channels through which the vital energy circulates throughout the body. All illnesses are believed to result from an imbalance or blockage of this flow.

Meridian stretching Stretching exercises designed to encourage physical and mental flexibility, for the body and mind to perform at their peak. Combines exercise, yoga and traditional Chinese medicine.

Microdermabrasion Clinical skin-resurfacing procedure where a jet of fine crystals is vacuumed across the surface of the face to remove the topmost layer of skin.

Milk Rich source of calcium, protein and vitamins necessary for healthy growth and development. Fermented to produce cheese and yoghurt. In skincare, used in the form of cleansing and moisturizing milk baths to improve skin tone and texture.

Mineralize Supply of minerals to the body.

Moor mud wrap Treatment with moor mud, which has anti-inflammatory and astringent properties ideal for detoxification and treatment of arthritic and skin ailments as well as hormonal and fertility problems.

Moroccan Mint Tea A brew of green and mint leaves. Ideal refresher for the hot, dry North African climate.

Moxibustion Burning of the dried herb moxa around the acupoints to relieve pain. Cones of moxa are applied either directly onto the skin, or indirectly with an insulating layer of other herbs.

Mud pool Pool with a central pedestal of volcanic mud. The mud is self-applied to the body and left to dry in the sun before being rinsed off leaving the skin deeply cleansed.

Mud treatment Mineral-rich mud used to detoxify, loosen muscles and stimulate circulation.

Mukh Lepa An ayurvedic facial treatment.

Myofacial release Use of the fingers, palms, forearms and elbows in long, deliberate, gliding strokes to stretch and mobilize the fascia (connective tissue that surrounds and supports the muscles, organs and bones) to provide long-term relief of pain and promote well-being.

Nail art Beautification of the nails with patterns, paintings or other decorative motifs.

Nasya Use of nasal medicated drops to clear the nasal passages to help allergies. One of the five purification techniques in panchakarma.

Naturopathy Holistic approach that believes in the body's ability to heal itself. Uses treatments not to alleviate symptoms, but to encourage the body's self-healing mechanism. Symptoms are viewed not as a part of the illness, but as the body's way of ridding itself of the problem. Also known as natural medicine.

Njavarakizhi Ayurvedic massage using small linen bags—filled with rice cooked in milk mixed with a herbal blend—to induce sweat. Applied with medicated oil. Strengthens and rejuvenates.

Nutritional consultation Consultation with a qualified nutritional practitioner to review eating habits and dietary needs. Taking into account your lifestyle, food intolerance, appetite control and weight goals, the nutritionist may compile a nutritionally balanced programme to help you attain optimal health and weight.

Onsen Japanese natural hot springs.

Organic food Food grown without the use of pesticides or other chemicals.

Ovo lacto vegetarian Vegan who consumes milk and egg products.

Ovo vegetarian Vegan who consumes egg products.

Panchakarma Ayurvedic therapy (vamana, virechana, vasti, nasya and raktamokshana) that helps rid the body of its toxins.

Paraffin treatment Application of warm paraffin wax on the hands and feet to the skin to absorb toxins. Leaves the skin silky soft.

Pedicure Treatment that beautifies the feet and nails. Feet are soaked and exfoliated with a scrub to remove dead skin cells, cuticles are groomed, and nails are trimmed and shaped. Nails may be buffed to a shine or coated with a polish. May include a foot and calf massage.

Pediluve Treatment in which feet and legs are dipped in alternate tubs of bubbling jets of warm and cold seawater to improve blood circulation.

Pelotherapy The use of mud in packs, wraps or baths for the medicinal treatment of rheumatic, skin and digestive ailments.

Personal fitness assessment Programme that assesses your current fitness levels to recommend a suitable exercise programme. May include tests for aerobic capacity, body composition, blood pressure, heart rate, and muscular endurance and strength.

Personal training One-on-one personalized workout with a qualified instructor.

Pescetarian Vegetarian who consumes fish.

Physiotherapy Rehabilitative therapy that helps recovery from injury, surgery or disease. Treatments—which include massage, traction, hydrotherapy, corrective exercise and electrical stimulation—help to relieve pain, increase strength and improve the range of motion.

Pilates Exercise comprising slow, precise movements with special exercise equipment that engage the body and mind, and increase flexibility and strength without building bulk.

Pizhichil Ayurvedic massage in which lukewarm herbal oils are gently and rhythmically applied to the body by two to four therapists.

Pregnancy massage Pre-natal massage that deals with the special needs of a mother-to-be, and anti-natal massages that deal with her needs after she has delivered. Some spas have massage tables with a hole in the centre to accommodate a pregnant woman.

Pressotherapy Computerized pressure massage that uses a specially designed airbag that compresses and deflates to improve the circulation throughout the feet and legs.

Purvakarma Two Ayurvedic treatments (snehana and svedana) that soften and cleanse the skin in preparation for panchakarma.

Qi gong Chinese physical exercise of working with or mastering qi. Uses breathing and body movement to help develop a powerful qi.

Qi 'Vital energy' or 'life force' of the universe and the body. Also known as ki (Japanese) and prana (Indian).

Raktamokshana Blood purification treatment for illnesses such as skin problems using surgical instruments or leeches. One of the five purification techniques in panchakarma.

Rasul Traditional Arabian cleansing ritual performed in a Tiled steam room in which different muds are applied to the body before being washed off. Often used as pre-massage treatment in the modern day.

Reflexology Application of finger-point pressure to reflex zones on the feet—and to a lesser extent, hands—to improve circulation, ease pain, relax the body and re-establish the flow of energy through the body. Its underlying theory is that specific areas on the feet and hands correspond with specific body parts, organs and glands, and that the manipulation of specific areas can bring about change associated with the corresponding parts.

Reiki Healing technique based on ancient Tibetan teachings. The practitioner places his palms over or on various areas of the body for a few minutes each to energize and balance the body, mind and spirit. Helps treat physical problems, heal emotional stresses and encourage personal transformation.

Rosewater and rose essential oil Aromatherapy essences widely used in skincare for dry, sensitive or ageing skin, to diminish enlarged facial capillaries and act as an antiseptic for eye irritations. The oil contains cleansing, purifying and anti-depressant properties and also aids in regulating the menstrual cycle.

Saffron Spice harvested from the crocus sativus plant and added to recipes for flavour and aroma. Long used in ayurvedic medicine to alleviate various disorders and lack of vitality. Today it is also valued for is relaxant, anti-oxidant and possibly, anti-carcinogenic properties.

Salt scrub Exfoliating treatment where the body is rubbed with a mixture of coarse salt and essential oils to remove dry, dead skin cells and stimulate circulation.

Samana Ayurvedic herbal medicine that works to balance the doshas.

Sauna Dry heat, wood-lined treatment room. The heat brings on sweating to help cleanse the body of impurities and relax the muscles. Usually followed by a cold plunge or shower.

Senna A small shrub native to the upper Nile regions of Africa and the Arabian peninsula. Its leaves and seeds are processed into crushed herbs and tea, which are commonly consumed as a laxative.

Shiatsu Massage that uses finger pressure-and also the hands, forearms, elbows, knees and feet-on acupoints. Calms and relaxes.

Shirodhara Ayurvedic massage in which warmed medicated oil steadily drips on the forehead, or the third eye. Relieves mental tension and calms the mind.

Signature treatment Treatment specially created by a spa or spa group, often using indigenous ingredients.

Sivananda A form of yoga based on the 12 sun salutation postures.

Shirovasthi Ayurvedic treatment in which warm herbal medicated oil is massaged on to the head after which a closely fitted cap is worn for a while to retain the therapeutic benefits of the oil.

Snehana Ayurvedic oil therapy in which a mixture of herbs, oils and natural ingredients are massaged on to the body. The oils may also be taken orally or introduced as enemas. One of the two preparatory treatments in purvakarma.

Spa Term, originating from the name of a town in Belgium where people flocked to in the 17th century for its healing waters, that refers to anything from a mineral spring to an establishment which provides facilities and services that helps you achieve a sense of well-being. Many spas also provide fitness activities, classes on well-being and spa cuisine. Types of spas include day spas (spas for day use); hotel or resort spas (spas located within hotels or resorts); destination spas (spas with an all-round emphasis on a healthy lifestyle, and include on-site accommodation, treatments, programmes and spa cuisine); and mineral springs spas (spas with a natural source of mineral or thermal waters, or seawater).

Spa cuisine Light, healthy meals served at spas. Typically low in calories, fat and salt.

Spa menu Selection of treatments and therapies offered by a spa.

Spa package Two or more treatments offered together. Often longer in length and good value.

Sports massage Deep tissue massage directed at muscles used in athletic activities to help the body achieve its maximum physical efficiency. Before physical exertion, it buffers against pain and injury; after, it helps remove lactic acid and restore muscle tone and range of movement.

Steaming Use of hot steam—often infused with essential oils or herbs—to relax the body, soften the skin, and open up the pores to prepare the face or body for treatment. Hair may also be steamed by wrapping it in a hot towel or exposing it to steam.

Steam room Tiled room with benches in which steam is generated at high pressure and temperature. The steam opens the pores, eliminates toxins, cleanses the skin and relaxes the body.

Step aerobics Aerobic sessions done with a small platform for stepping up and down.

Stone therapy Massage where hot, warm or cold smooth stones are rubbed in long, flowing strokes on to the oiled body, then placed on energy points to ease away tension. Also known as hot stone massage or la stone® therapy.

Stress management Techniques to deal with stress and anxiety.

Stretching Flexibility workout where various parts of the body are stretched by assuming different positions. Helps increase flexibility, and relieve stress and tension.

Svedana Body purification method to cleanse and relax through sweat therapy. One of the two preparatory treatments in purvakarma.

Swedish massage Massage in which oils are applied to the body with techniques such as gliding, kneading, rubbing, tapping and shaking. Relieves stress, tension and muscle pain; improves circulation; increases flexibility; and induces relaxation.

Tai chi Graceful movement that combines mental concentration with deep, controlled breathing. Regular practice brings about relaxation and good health. Stimulates the body's energy systems and enhances mental functions.

Tantra A form of yoga that includes visualization, chanting, asana and strong breathing practices.

Thai herbal massage Massage using a warmed pouch of steamed Thai herbs pressed against the body's meridians.

Thai massage Traditional massage of Thailand, influenced by Chinese and Indian healing arts, that involves a combination of stretching and gentle rocking, and uses a range of motions and acupressure techniques. The massage is oil-free, and performed on a traditional Thai mattress on the floor. Loose clothing is worn.

Thalassotherapy Treatments that harness mineral- and vitamin-rich seawater and seaweed for curative and preventive purposes. True thalassotherapy centres are located no more than 800 metres (2,625 feet) from the shore, and constantly pump fresh seawater filtered through large canals for use in the treatments.

Thermal bath Therapeutic use of thermal water rich in salts and minerals.

Traditional Chinese medicine (TCM) Holistic system of care that sees the body and mind as a whole. Treatments include herbal medicine, physical and mental exercises, and

therapies such as acupuncture and moxibustion.

Treatments for couples Typically treatments that a couple can enjoy together with a therapist pampering each person. Treatments specially designed for couples usually use an aphrodisiac blend of essential oils.

Tui na Chinese system of manual therapy used to treat specific illnesses of an internal nature and musculoskeletal ailments. Principal hand strokes include pushing (tui), grasping (na), pressing (an), rubbing (mo), rolling (gun), pulling (qian), beating (da) and shaking (dou). The hands, arms, elbows and feet may be used.

Turkish bath Series of hot and humid steam rooms, each of which increases in heat. You spend several minutes in each room and finish with a cool shower.

Vamana The consumption of potions to induce vomiting to treat bronchitis, and throat, chest and heart problems. One of the five purification techniques in panchakarma.

Vasti Use of enemas to calm nerves and treat fatigue, dry skin and digestive imbalances. One of the five purification techniques in panchakarma.

Vegan Person who exclusively consumes a vegetable and fruit diet, and does not eat animal products such as butter, cheese, eggs and milk.

Vegetarian Person who consumes mainly vegetables, fruit, nuts, pulses and grains, and who does not eat meat or fish, but eats animal products such as butter, cheese, eggs and milk.

Vichy shower Spray of water from five micro-jets fixed to a horizontal rail which rain down on you while you lie on a table below. May also include a massage. Also known as affusion shower or rain shower.

Vietnamese massage Invigorating massage that uses a combination of deep strokes and percussive movements. Benefits include stimulating the blood and lymphatic

circulation, improving the skin texture and tone, and warming muscle tissue.

Virechana Drinking a herb tea to help flush out elements that may clog the digestive tract. One of the five purification techniques in panchakarma.

Visualization Technique that involves focusing the mind by consciously creating a mental image of a desired condition to bring about change. May be self-directed or therapist guided. Also known as imaging.

Watsu Therapy where you float in a swimming pool, supported by a therapist who manipulates your body with stretches, rhythmic movements and pressure point massage to bring deep relaxation.

Waxing Temporary hair removal method. Warm or cool wax, usually honeycomb blended with oils, is applied on to areas of unwanted hair. A cloth is smoothed on to the area and quickly whisked off, pulling the hair off with the wax.

Wet area Area in a spa where Jacuzzis, saunas, cold tubs, hot tubs, steam baths and pressure showers are located.

Whirlpool Hot bath with high-pressure jets on the sides and bottom that circulate the water. Massages muscles and relaxes the body.

Whitening treatment Treatment that brightens the skin, restores lost radiance and tones pigmentation marks.

Yin and yang Yin is the universal energy force whose characteristics are feminine, cold, dark, quiet, static and wet. Yang is masculine, warm, bright, dynamic and dry. In traditional Chinese medicine, true balance and health are achieved when these two opposing forces are in balance. Also known as in and yo (Japanese).

Yoga Ancient Hindu practice comprising focused deep breathing, and stretching and toning the body using various postures (asanas). The ultimate goal is to reach your full physical, mental and spiritual potential. Relaxes, and improves circulation, flexibility and strength.

Spa Directory

KINGDOM OF BAHRAIN

Banyan Tree Al Areen
PO Box 18108
Manama
Kingdom of Bahrain
Tel: (973) 17 558 455
Fax: (973) 17 550 638
Email: reservations@banyantree.com
Website: www.banyantree.com

The Ritz-Carlton Bahrain Hotel & Spa
PO Box 55577
Manama
Kingdom of Bahrain
Tel: (973) 17 580 000
Fax: (973) 17 580 333
Website: www.ritzcarlton.com

EGYPT

Aswan

Elephantine Island Resort Aswan operated by Mövenpick
Elephantine Island
PO Box 62
Aswan
Egypt
Tel: (20) 97 230 3455
Fax: (20) 97 231 3538
Email: resort.aswan@moevenpick.com
Website: www.moevenpick-hotels.com

Cairo

The Spa & Wellness Centre (pp 116–117)
Four Seasons Hotel Cairo at The First Residence
35 Giza Street
Giza, Cairo
Egypt 12311
Tel: (20) 2 573 1212
Fax: (20) 2 568 1616
Email: nada.ismail@fourseasons.com
Website: www.fourseasons.com

Four Seasons Hotel Cairo at Nile Plaza (pp 118–119)
1089 Corniche El Nil
PO Box 63 Maglis El Shaab

Garden City, Cairo
Egypt 11519
Tel (20) 2 791 7000
Fax (20) 2 791 6900
Email: reservations.cai@fourseasons.com
Website: www.fourseasons.com

El Quseir

Mövenpick Resort El Quseir
Sirena Beach
El Quadim Bay
El Quseir
Egypt
Tel: (20) 65 333 2100
Fax: (20) 65 333 2128
Email: resort.quseir@moevenpick.com
Website: www.moevenpick-hotels.com

El Gouna

Mövenpick Resort & Spa El Gouna
PO Box 72
Hurghada
123456 El Gouna
Red Sea, Egypt
Tel: (20) 65 354 4501
Fax: (20) 65 354 5160
Email: resort.elgouna@moevenpick.com
Website: www.moevenpick-hotels.com

Hurghada

Oberoi Sahl Hasheesh
Red Sea
Egypt
Tel: (20) 65 344 0777
Fax: (20) 65 344 0788
Email: toshgm@oberoi.com.eg
Website: www.oberoihotels.com

La Residence Des Cascades Golf Resort & Thalasso
Hurghada PO Box 403
Soma Bay
Red Sea
Egypt
Tel: (20) 65 354 2333
Fax: (20) 65 354 2933
Email: info@residencedescascades.com
Website: www.somabay.com

Sharm El Shiekh

Four Seasons Resort Sharm El Sheikh (pp 120–121)
One Four Seasons Boulevard
PO Box 203
Sharm El Sheikh
South Sinai, Egypt
Tel: (20) 69 360 3555
Fax: (20) 69 360 3550
Email: daniela.steiner@fourseasons.com
Website: www.fourseasons.com

Hyatt Regency Sharm El Sheikh (pp 122–123)
The Gardens Bay
PO Box 58
Sharm El Sheikh
South Sinai, Egypt
Tel: (20) 69 360 1234
Fax: (20) 69 360 3600
Email: sharm@hyattintl.com
Website: www.sharm.hyatt.com

The Ritz Carlton Sharm El Sheikh Resort
Om El Seed Peninsula
PO Box 72
Sharm El Sheikh
South Sinai, Egypt
Tel: (20) 69 3 661919
Fax: (20) 69 3 661920
Website: www.ritzcarlton.com

Sheraton Sharm Hotel, Resort & Villas
Al Pasha Coast
Sharm El Sheikh
South Sinai, Egypt
Tel: (20) 69 3602070
Fax: (20) 69 3602099
Email: reservationssharmegypt@sheraton.com
Website: www.sheraton.com

Taba

Mövenpick Resort Taba
PO Box 14, 46621 Taba
South Sinai, Egypt
Tel: (20) 69 3530 530
Fax: (20) 69 3530 540
Email: resort.taba@moevenpick.com
Website: www.moevenpick-hotels.com

JORDAN

Amman
Four Seasons
5th Circle
Al-Kindi Street
Jabal Amman
Jordan
Tel: (962) 6 550 5555
Fax: (962) 6 550 5556
Website: www.fourseasons.com

Kempinski
Abdul Hameed Shouman Street, Shmeisani
PO Box 941045
11194 Amman
Jordan
Tel: (962) 6 520 0200
Fax: (962) 6 520 0202
Email: reservations.amman@kempinski.com
Website: www.kempinski.com

Mercure Ma'In Thermal Spa Hotel Jordan
801 Madaba
Jordan
Tel: (962) 5 324 5550
Fax: (962) 5 324 5500
Email: H2174@accor-hotels.com

Dead Sea
Jordan Valley Marriott Resort & Spa (pp 128–129)
PO Box 928417
11190 Amman
Jordan
Tel: (962) 5 356 0400
Fax: (962) 5 356 0444
Email: jordanvalley@marriotthotels.com
Website: www.marriott.com

Zara Spa at the Mövenpick Resort & Spa
(pp 124–127)
PO Box 815538
11180 Amman
Jordan
Tel: (962) 5 356 1111
Fax: (962) 5 356 1125
Email: zaraspa@movenpick-deadsea.com
Website: www.zaraspa.com

KUWAIT

Hilton Kuwait Resort & Spa
PO Box 7887
Fahaheel
64009
Kuwait
Tel: (965) 372 5500
Fax: (965) 372 8130
Email: kuwait@hilton.com
Website: www.hilton.com

JW Marriott Hotel Kuwait City
PO Box 1216
Al Shuhada Street
Safat
13124
Kuwait
Tel: (965) 245 5550
Fax: (965) 243 8391
Website: www.marriott.com

Kempinski Julai'a Hotel & Resort
King Fahad Highway
Exit 245
Julai'a
PO Box 488
Sabahiya
54575
Kuwait
Tel: (965) 844 444
Fax: (965) 328 3601
Website: www.kempinski-kuwait.com

LEBANON

Beirut
Intercontinental Phoenicia Beirut
Minet el Hosn
Beirut
Lebanon
Tel: (961) 1 369 100
Fax: (961) 1 369 101
Email: phoenicia@phoenicia-ic.com
Website: www.ichotelsgroup.com

Metropolitan Palace Hotel Beirut
PO Box 5555

Horch Tabet
Sin El Fil
Beirut
Lebanon
Tel: (961) 1 496 666
Fax: (961) 1 502 502
Email: beirutpalace@methotels.com
Website: www.methotels.com

Mövenpick Hotel & Resort Beirut
General de Gaulle Avenue
PO Box 2038 6908
000 Beirut
Lebanon
Tel: (961) 1 869 666
Fax: (961) 1 809 326
Email: resort.beirut@moevenpick.com
Website: www.moevenpick-hotels.com

Sheraton Coral Beach
PO Box 13-5050,
Jnah Avenue
Beirut
Lebanon
Tel: (961) 1 859 000
Fax: (961) 1 859 026
Email: coralbeach.reservations@sheraton.com
Website: www.sheraton.com

Broumana
Grand Hills Hotel & Spa (pp 130–131)
Al Charkiah Road
Broumana
Lebanon
Tel: (961) 4 862 888
Fax: (961) 4 861 888
Email: info@grandhillsvillage.com
Website: www.grandhillsvillage.com

Kfardebiane
InterContinental Mountain Resort & Spa Mzaar
Ouyoun El Simane
Kfardebiane
Lebanon
Tel: (961) 9 340 100
Fax: (961) 9 340 101
Email: mzaar@interconti.com
Website: www.interconti.com

SULTANATE OF OMAN

Al Bustan Palace InterContinental Muscat
PO Box 1998
114 Muttrah
Sultanate of Oman
Tel: (968) 24 799 666
Fax: (968) 24 799 600
Email: albustan@albustanpalace.com
Website: www.al-bustan.intercontinental.com

The Spa at the Chedi (pp 132–133)
The Chedi, Muscat
PO Box 964, Post Code 133
Muscat
Sultanate of Oman
Tel: (968) 24 524 400
Fax: (968) 24 493 485
Email: spa@chedimuscat.com
Website: www.ghmotels.com

CHI Spa at Shangri-La's Barr Al Jissah Resort &
Spa (pp 134–135)
PO Box 644, PC 113
Muscat
Sultanate of Oman
Tel: (968) 24 776 666
Fax: (968) 24 776 677
Email: slmu@shangri-la.com
Website: www.shangri-la.com/spa

QATAR

Four Seasons Hotel Doha (pp 136–137)
The Corniche
PO Box 24665
Doha, Qatar
Tel: (974) 494 8888
Fax: (974) 494 8282
Email: spa.doh@fourseasons.com
Website: www.fourseasons.com

Doha Marriott Hotel
Doha PO Box 1911
Doha, Qatar
Tel: (974) 4 298 888
Fax: (974) 4 418 784
Website: www.marriott.com

Ritz-Carlton Doha
PO Box 23400
Doha
Qatar
Tel: (974) 484 8000
Fax: (974) 484 8484
Website: www.ritzcarlton.com

Sheraton Doha Hotel & Resort
PO Box 600, Al Corniche Street
Doha
Qatar
Tel: (974) 485 4444
Fax: (974) 483 2323
Email: sheraton.doha@sheraton.com
Website: www.sheraton.com

SAUDI ARABIA

Al Faisaliah Hotel
PO Box 4148, King Fahad Road
Olaya, Riyadh 11491
Kingdom of Saudi Arabia
Tel: (966) 1 273 2000
Fax: (966) 1 273 2001
Email: alfaisaliah@rosewoodhotels.com
Website: www.alfaisaliahhotel.com

Four Seasons Hotel Riyadh
Kingdom Centre
PO Box 231000, Riyadh
Kingdom of Saudi Arabia 11321
Tel: (966) 1 211 5000
Fax: (966) 1 211 5001
Website: www.fourseasons.com

Sunset Beach Resort
PO Box 272, 31952 Alkhobar
Kingdom of Saudi Arabia
Website: www.sunset-beach.com.sa

SYRIA

Safir Al-Sayedah Zeinab Hotel
PO Box 684
Damascus
Syria
Tel: (963) 11 647 0140

Fax: (963) 11 647 0131
Email: safir-zeinab@mail.sy
Website: www.safirhotels.com

TUNISIA

Mövenpick Ulysse Palace & Thalasso
(pp 138–141)
Route Touristique
Plage de Sidi Mehrez, BP 239
4128 Djerba
Tunisia
Tel: (216) 75 758 777
Fax: (216) 75 757 850
Email: resort.djerba@moevenpick.com
Website: www.moevenpick-hotels.com

UNITED ARAB EMIRATES

Abu Dhabi
Emirates Palace Abu Dhabi
PO Box 39999
Abu Dhabi
UAE
Tel: (971) 2 690 9000
Fax: (971) 2 690 9999
Email: info.emiratespalace@kempinski.com
Website: www.emiratespalace.com

InterContinental Abu Dhabi
PO Box 4171, Al Khalidya Street
Abu Dhabi
UAE
Tel: (971) 2 666 6888
Fax: (971) 2 666 9153
Email: abudhabi@icauh.ae
Website: www.abu-dhabi.intercontinental.com

DUBAI

Angsana Spa Arabian Ranches, Dubai
311, Emirates Road
Dubai
UAE
Tel: (971) 4 361 8251
Fax: (971) 4 361 8252
Email: spa-arabianranches@angsana.com
Website: www.angsanaspa.com

Angsana Spa & Health Club Dubai Marina
Level 2, Marina Walk,
Dubai Marina
UAE
Tel: (971) 4 368 4356
Fax: (971) 4 368 3256
Email: spa-dubaimarina@angsana.com
Website: www.angsanaspa.com

Assawan Spa at Burj Al Arab (pp 146–149)
PO Box 74147
Dubai
UAE
Tel: (971) 4 301 7338
Fax: (971) 4 301 7318
Email: BAAassawan@jumeirah.com
Website: www.jumeirah.com

Aviation Club
P. O. Box 55400
Dubai
UAE
Tel: (971) 4 282 4122
Fax: (971) 4 282 4751
Email: info@aviationclub.ae
Website: www.aviationclub.ae

Al Asala Spa
Dubai Ladies Club
PO Box 72212
Dubai
UAE
Tel: (971) 4 349 9922
Fax: (971) 4 349 9955
Website: www.dubailadiesclub.com

Caracalla Spa
Le Royal Meridien Beach Resort & Spa, Dubai
PO Box 24970
Dubai
UAE
Tel: (971) 4 399 5555
Fax: (971) 4 399 5999
Website: www.royaldubai.lemeridien.com

Cleopatra's Spa (pp 150–151)
Pyramid's Health and Leisure
Wafi City

Dubai
UAE
Tel: (971) 4 324 7700/0000
Fax: (971) 4 324 4611
Website: www.waficity.com

Dubai Marine Spa
Dubai Marine Beach Resort & Spa
PO Box 5182
Dubai
UAE
Tel: (971) 4 346 1111
Fax: (971) 4 346 0234
Email: spa@dxbmarine.com
Website: www.dxbmarine.com

The Grand Spa at the Grand Hyatt (pp 152–153)
Atrium Level
Grand Hyatt Dubai
PO Box 7978
Dubai
UAE
Tel: (971) 4 317 2333
Fax (971) 4 317 1235
Email: dubai.grand@hyattintl.com
Website: www.dubai.grand.hyatt.com

Habtoor Grand Resort & Spa
PO Box 24454
Dubai
UAE
Tel: (971) 4 399 5000
Fax: (971) 4 399 4547
Email: grandjumeirah@habtoorhotels.com
Website: www.habtoorhotels.com

Jamilah Spa & Leisure Centre at Al Maha Desert Resort & Spa (pp 142–145)
PO Box 7631
Dubai
UAE
Tel: (971) 4 303 4222
Fax: (971) 4 343 9696
Email: almaha@emirates.com
Website: www.al-maha.com

Jebel Ali Golf Resort & Spa (pp 154–155)
PO Box 9255

Dubai
UAE
Tel: (971) 4 883 6000
Fax: (971) 4 883 5543
Email: jagrs@jaihotels.com
Website: www.jebelali-international.com

Jumeirah Emirates Towers
PO Box 72127
Dubai
UAE
Tel: (971) 4 330 0000
Fax: (971) 4 330 3030
Email: JETinfo@jumeirah.com
Website: www.jumeirahemiratestowers.com

Natural Elements
Le Meridien Dubai
PO Box 10001
Airport Road
Dubai
UAE
Tel: (971) 4 282 4040
Fax: (971) 4 282 5540
Website: dubai.lemeridien.com

One&Only Royal Mirage, Dubai Residence & Spa (pp 164–167)
PO Box 37252
Dubai
UAE
Tel: (971) 4 399 9999
Fax: (971) 4 399 9998
Email: info@oneandonlyroyalmirage.ae
Website: www.oneandonlyresorts.com

Park Hyatt Dubai (pp168–171)
PO Box 2822
Dubai
UAE
Tel: (971) 4 602 1234
Fax: (971) 4 602 1235
Email: dubai.park@hyattintl.com
Website: www.dubai.park.hyatt.com

Retreat
Grosvenor House
Grosvenor House Dubai

PO Box 118500
Dubai
UAE
Tel: (971) 4 399 8888
Fax: (971) 4 399 8444
Website: grosvenorhouse.lemeridien.com

The Ritz-Carlton Spa
Ritz-Carlton Dubai Resort & Spa
PO Box 26525
Dubai
UAE
Tel: (971) 4 399 4000
Fax: (971) 4 399 4309
Website: www.ritzcarlton.com

Satori Spa
Jumeirah Bab Al Shams Desert Resort & Spa
PO Box 8168
Dubai
UAE
Tel: (971) 4 832 6699
Fax: (971) 4 832 6698
Email: BASfeedback@jumeirah.com
Website: www.jumeirahinternational.com

Satori Spa
Jumeirah Beach Club Resort & Spa
PO BOX 26878
Dubai
UAE
Tel: (971) 4 3445333
Fax: (971) 4 3446222
Email: JBCinfo@jumeirah.com
Website: www.jumeirahinternational.com

Sensasia Urban Spa
Upper Level, The Village,
Jumeirah Beach Road
PO Box 71393
Dubai
UAE
Tel: (971) 4349 8850
Email: info@sensasiaspas.com
Website: htwww.sensasiaspas.com

The Health Club & Spa at Shangri-La (pp 172–173)
Shangri-La Dubai

Sheikh Zayed Road
PO Box 75880
Dubai
UAE
Tel: (971) 4 405 2441/2447
Fax: (971) 4 343 8886
Email: sldb.spa@shangri-la.com
Website: www.shangri-la.com

Six Senses Spa (pp 156–163)
Madinat Jumeirah
PO Box 75157
Dubai
UAE
Tel: (971) 4 366 6818
Fax: (971) 4 366 6800
Email: sixsensesspa@madinatjumeirah.com
Website: www.madinatjumeirah.com

Taj Spa
The Taj Palace Hotel, Dubai
PO Box 42211,
Dubai
UAE.
Tel: (971) 4 223 2222
Fax: (971) 4 227 8222
Email: tphreservations.dxb@tajhotels.com
Website: www.tajhotels.com

Willow Stream Spa
The Fairmount Dubai
PO Box 97555
Sheikh Zayed Road
Dubai
UAE
Tel: (971) 4 332 5555
Fax: (971) 4 332 4555
Email: dubai@fairmont.com
Website: www.fairmont.com

Fujairah
Le Meridien Al Aqah Beach Resort, Fujairah
PO Box 3070
Fujairah
UAE
Tel: (971) 9 244 9000
Fax: (971) 9 244 9001
Website: www.alaqah.lemeridien.com

Sharjah
Dalouk Spa Sharjah Ladies Club (pp 174–177)
Sharjah
UAE
Tel: (971) 6564 6663
Fax: (971) 6565 7799
Email: dalouk@sharjahladiesclub.com
Website: www.sharjahladiesclub.com

Millennium Hotel Sharjah
PO Box 3930, Corniche Road
Sharjah
UAE
Tel: (971) 6 556 6666
Fax: (971) 6 556 0999
Email: sales.sharjah@mill-cop.com
Website: www.millenniumhotels.com

Radisson SAS Resort Hotel
PO Box 3527
Sharjah
UAE
Tel: (971) 6 565 7777
Fax: (971) 6 565 7276
Email: Sales.Sharjah@RadissonSAS.com
Website: www.radissonsas.com

Umm Al Quwain
Imar Spa
PO Box : 2040
Umm Al Quwain
UAE
Tel : (971) 6 7664440
Fax: (971) 6 7664443
Email: imarspa@emirates.net.ae
Website: www.imarspa.com

YEMEN

Sheraton Gold Mohur Hotel & Resort
PO Box 13040
Hai Althawra
Aden
Yemen
Tel: (967) 2 204 010
Fax: (967) 2 205 158
Email: reservations.aden.yemen@sheraton.com
Website: www.sheraton.com

Bibliography

Cressey, Susan, *The Beauty Therapy Fact File*, 3rd Edition, Butterworth-Heinemann, Oxford, 1998

Crebbin-Bailey, Jane, Harcup, John and Harrington, John, *The Spa Book: The Official Guide to Spa Therapy*, Thomson Learning, London, 2005

Fischer-Rizzi, Susanne, *Complete Aromatherapy Handbook: Essential Oils for Radiant Health*, Sterling Publishing Company, New York, 1990

Irwin, Neil, *Crystals*, Thorsons, London, 1991

Leavy, Hannelore and Bergel, Reinhard, *The Spa Encyclopedia: A Guide to Treatments & Their Benefits for Health and Healing*, Delmar Learning a division of Thomson Learning, New York, 2003

Lee, Ginger, *Spa Style Europe: Therapies, Cuisines, Spas*, Thames & Hudson, London, 2004; Archipelago Press an imprint of Editions Didier Millet, Singapore, 2004

Mallos, Tess, *The Complete Middle East Cookbook*, Weldon Publishing, NSW Australia, 1990

Mernagh-Ward, Dawn and Cartwright, Jennifer, *Health and Beauty Therapy*, Nelson Thornes Ltd, Cheltenham, 2001

Murray, Michael, Pizzorno, Joseph, Pizzorno, Lara, *The Encyclopedia of Healing Foods*, Atria Books, New York, 2005

Napier, Eloise, *A Place to Spa: Exceptional Destination Spas from Around the World*, Conran Octopus Ltd, London, 2002

Norris, Stephanie, *Secrets of Colour Healing*, Dorling Kindersley, London, 2001

O'Brien, Kate, *Spa Style Asia-Pacific: Therapies, Cuisines, Spas*, Thames & Hudson, London, 2006; Editions Didier Millet, Singapore, 2006

Sullivan, Karen, *Natural Remedies: An Essential A-Z Guide*, Starfire, London, 2001

Picture Credits

Index